What Would You Do?

# A Time to Belong

By Vicki Grove

D1023919

Teenage BOOKS

Group

Loveland, Colorado

# Dedication

For Adonna,
my best friend.

## A Time to Belong
Copyright © 1990 by Vicki Grove

First Printing

**Credits**
Edited by Michael D. Warden
Cover and book designed by Judy Atwood Bienick
Cover and illustrations by Rand Kruback

**Library of Congress Cataloging-in-Publication Data**
Grove, Vicki.
    A time to belong / by Vicki Grove.
      p. cm.
    Summary: As sixteen-year-old Ann, the reader makes decisions controlling the course of her life and her behavior in such areas as friendship, peer pressure, self-esteem, moral issues, and faith in God.
    ISBN 1-55945-051-7
    1. Plot-your-own stories. [1. Christian life—Fiction. 2. Plot-your-own stories.] I. Title.
PZ7.G9275T1 1990
[Fic]—dc20                             90-36320
                                               CIP
                                               AC

Printed in the United States of America

# Your Road Map

Some things in life just seem to happen to you—getting the flu, for instance. Or having a flat tire on the way to a big date. Or on the bright side, finding a $10 bill in the sand on the beach.

But other things—probably more things than we're willing to admit—really are within our control. You *can* avoid that D in geometry by turning down the radio and studying more. A radical idea, sure, but true nonetheless.

It all comes down to choices.

Friendship is one of those many things that's choice-directed. It doesn't often just "happen." The vast majority of friendships take planning and need control. Oh, sure, people will sometimes "fall" into your life and friendship will blossom without much effort on either side. But maintaining that friendship always takes work.

Some friendships turn out to be some of the best experiences of your life. Others may be painful. To a great extent you have the power and the responsibility to consciously direct the course of each friendship you choose to make. And the decisions you make directly affect how healthy or unhealthy your friendship will become.

*A Time to Belong* is about a 16-year-old girl named Ann. She faces many friendship decisions, which you'll make for her. Start reading at the beginning. Then when you reach a decision point, choose how you want Ann to decide and turn to the page that's indicated. You can read the book dozens of times without repeating the same story.

But be careful! A decision that may seem trivial at the moment may have significant results. A choice that seems clear on an intellectual or physical level may be disastrous on a spiritual or emotional level. And some decisions may lead to events that are out of Ann's control.

As you read, step back occasionally. Look at things from all angles. Listen to the advice Ann hears from her friends, family and mentors. And, of course, from God.

Like everything worth having, friendship isn't always easy. Not for Ann, not for you, not for me. But really—if it was simple, would we value it as highly?

Go in peace with God. And with each other.

# A Time to Belong

"Ta dum!" Ann clicked off the griddle and carried her heaping platter of pancakes to the table as proudly as if they were studded with diamonds instead of blueberries. "Okay, dig in, Mom, and don't bother with compliments to the chef. Just leave a big tip and I'll get the idea."

"These look delicious, Annie," Mom laughed. "Boy, it's sure nice to be treated to Saturday breakfast before work. What do you have planned today, after kitchen duty, that is?"

Ann's carefree mood suddenly drained away like the syrup from the bottle she held suspended over her plate.

"Oh, the usual," she murmured. "Cleaning, homework. Saturday stuff."

"Uh, listen, honey, you don't have to clean today. I only work 'til noon at the library, so I can start on that later. Why don't you have some friends over?" Mom's suggestion sounded a little too cheerful.

Ann's throat tightened. In the eight months since Mom's divorce had become final and they'd moved to Crestview, Ann's social life—or lack of one—had been the chief topic of conversation. Ann slammed the syrup bottle down on the table so hard her orange juice sloshed over.

"Mom, really, I can plan my own Saturday, okay?"

After a few long moments of silence, Mom shrugged and smiled. "Sure, honey. You know I'm only trying to help."

◼

In her room a while later, Ann sprawled on her bed and stared miserably at her posters. Sometimes the pictures of rainbows, flowery fields and waterfalls cheered her up when she was down, but today they just made her want to cry. Why couldn't the world really be beautiful and simple like that? Things must be pretty pathetic if your mother thinks she has to step in and try to force people to like you!

Why'd they have to move clear to Crestview anyway? And why now, when Ann was 16—easily the most confusing age she could remember? Back in Oregon, everybody was friends with everybody else. You didn't have to worry about people thinking you were weird if you said or did something wrong. No one worried about being popular or cool or having busy Saturdays. Or any of that stuff.

But deep inside she knew, to be honest, she had been just as self-conscious in Oregon as she was here in Missouri.

Why couldn't she be like Mom, who'd made tons of friends already? Mom didn't seem to spend any time at all agonizing over whether people liked her. They just did! It wasn't fair.

"Annie?" Mom's voice came up the stairs to cut into her gloomy musings. "I'm leaving for work. Have a good day, okay?"

"Okay," she mumbled listlessly, then flopped over on her stomach and hugged her pillow.

She was alone, at 9:00 on a beautiful spring Saturday morning. Alone, while probably every other kid in town was with other kids, laughing and goofing off and having fun at Crestview Mall or in Briarwood Park or at each other's houses.

She actually considered calling someone, though making the first move like that would take colossal nerve—more nerve than she'd ever managed to muster before. Linda Peterson, who sat next to her in algebra and sometimes borrowed her notes, didn't seem to have many other friends. Maybe she'd want to do something.

Or maybe one of the kids from youth group at church. A few of them had asked her to go out for a Coke after church a couple of times, but she hadn't gone because she felt too nervous, and she figured they'd just asked her out of sympathy anyway—since she was alone all the time.

Linda Peterson. Keri Jones, Cora Bagis or Rachelle Washington from youth group. The names ran over and over in her head, but she couldn't get up her courage to call.

When the phone rang, she nearly screamed. Didn't all Mom's friends know she worked Saturday mornings?

"Hello?"

"Hi, is this Ann? Ann Tyler?"

"Uh, yes, that's me."

"Hi, this is Tara Hastings. You probably don't remember me, but I'm the new girl that sits behind you in history."

"I ... I remember you," Ann said, bewildered. Tara had

moved from Chicago just the week before. She was one of those girls you knew would be immediately popular—cool, pretty and confident. What in the world was she calling Ann about?

"Ann, I was wondering ... could you possibly come over this morning? I'm behind on my schoolwork here, and I don't know anybody, and ... well, I need help."

Ann's heart was slamming. How incredible that Tara called just when Ann was thinking she'd do anything to be with someone this morning. But Tara was so cool! It'd be so scary being around her. What would they find in common to talk about?

Ann would definitely feel self-conscious around Tara. Wouldn't it be better to make up an excuse to stay home and avoid the whole thing? But then again, Ann wanted friends here so much!

## What would you do?

*If Ann agrees to go to Tara's, turn to page 50.*
*If she chickens out and stays home, turn to page 116.*

"Thanks," Ann said, taking the frosted bottle. She clumsily fiddled with the cap, hoping she could figure out how to open the thing without looking hopeless.

"So, what do you do for fun, Ann?" Tara asked as she easily opened her bottle and took a long, deep drink.

"Well, you know, I've got lots of school and home stuff. That takes a lot of time," Ann began, feeling flustered. Was this the point where Tara learned how inept she was socially, as well as where things like wine coolers were concerned? She gave the screw-top a big jerk, then fell limp with relief when it opened.

"Yeah, but what about night stuff? friend things?" Tara pressed. "Do you belong to any clubs or anything?"

"Well ... there's church. And youth group. I go to a lot of, well, activities with the kids there."

"Oh, yeah?" Tara commented, then laughed a little. "Like what kind of activities does this church of yours come up with?"

Ann stared hard at her bottle, not able to drink and not able to open up about her faith. Was that real interest she heard in Tara's voice or sarcasm?

---

## Blind choice:

*Without looking ahead, turn to page 12 or page 19 to continue the story.*

Ann threw the pillow across the room, jumped to her feet and dialed the phone before she could lose her nerve.

"Hello?"

"Tara? Hi, this is Ann Tyler again. Listen, uh, I'd like to come over today after all, if you still want me to, that is."

"Great! But I've got a better idea," Tara answered. "I really don't feel like hitting the books, so why don't we do something fun instead? I'll pick you up in an hour, and we can go to the mall. I need clothes desperately."

Ann spent that hour frantically changing into and out of every pair of jeans and every sweater she owned. For some reason it seemed crucial that she look just right, like somebody Tara would be proud to run around with. As she glanced in her vanity mirror for the zillionth time, her frantic eyes happened to settle on a tiny heart-shape sticker a Sunday school teacher had given her for her ninth or 10th birthday.

"Smile, God loves you!" she read now, and laughed as some nervousness drained from her. She even managed to breathe a tiny prayer. "Just help me remember that if I feel like a jerk today, Lord, okay? Amen."

When Tara honked outside, she was driving a hot red Mustang convertible. The top was down, and Tara's shining auburn hair blew around her head like a playful fire.

"This car's great!" Ann slid into the tiny cream-colored bucket seat beside Tara and yelled to be heard above the music blasting from the tape player. "Your parents'?"

"Mine," Tara said, sounding bored about it. "Now, which way to the best mall?"

Ann had been to Crestview Mall lots of times, of course, but being there with Tara was definitely a whole new experience. Tara was only interested in going into the most expensive clothing stores, places Ann had only seen from outside their tempting plate-glass windows. In Tarlinger's Leathers Tara left a pile of discarded skirts piled in the fitting room corner. She handled the suede purses in Saks Fifth Avenue like they were plastic toys and kept two disgruntled salesladies hopping in Yves St. Laurent.

Ann felt more and more uncomfortable, but Tara didn't seem to notice the irritated looks on the faces of the shop managers and salespeople. Ann began to wonder if she should ask Tara to go into different kinds of stores—ones selling the less expensive things that most of the kids were into. But would Tara get mad at that kind of suggestion?

## What would you do?

*If Ann plays along and doesn't say anything, turn to page 17.*
*If she decides to say something, turn to page 25.*

Ann put her drink down and took a deep breath.

"Well, we go out for pizza sometimes, and we have carwashes to raise money for good causes. Stuff like that. And we have neat discussions in youth group, conversations about choices, about problems. Like, well, drugs and alcohol. See, for instance—" Ann shrugged. "I don't drink. We've talked about it in youth group, and I decided it can definitely get too heavy."

To Ann's surprise and relief, Tara leaned toward her, looking really interested.

"I was in a group sort of like that back home in Chicago," she said. "It was neat, but I stopped going a year or so ago. Just sort of, I don't know, drifted out of it. Got busy with other things." Tara squinted off in the distance.

"You could come to our church tomorrow, then tomorrow night go to youth group with me," Ann said quickly before she could lose her nerve. "I mean, if you have time. The kids would love to get to know you."

Tara looked down and began to chew on her lip. "I don't know ..." But a few seconds later, she shrugged and smiled at Ann. "I haven't got anything else going on tomorrow, so why not?"

■

Sunday mornings were usually high stress times for Ann. She constantly wondered who was looking at her and what they must be thinking. And she was usually too shy to sit in the back of the sanctuary with the other kids during the worship service. So she stuck close to Mom. But that morning was different. With Tara beside her, it seemed only natural to join the other kids in holding down the senior high pew. There were a few brief introductions before the service began. Overall, the whole thing turned out to be a pleasant experience for both Tara and Ann.

Because things went so well that morning, Ann found herself looking forward to youth group all afternoon. Although, now that she thought about it, she supposed she'd taken youth group a little for granted lately. She'd been so nervous about how she looked and who would say what to her that she didn't really get into the discussions and planning like she should. Tonight, though, she decided she'd turn a corner on that. This weekend she'd start having confidence to act like someone who wanted friends—and could be one too.

■

Most everyone had arrived when Tara and Ann walked into the basement youth group room. Ann planned to introduce Tara first thing, but just as they were approaching the circle of kids sprawled on the old patchwork carpet near the pingpong table, Tara abruptly laughed.

"Wow, I can't believe this place! This looks just like the measly little nursery where the preschoolers met in my old church in Chicago. Aren't you guys into, you know, decorating and stuff?"

All conversations stopped instantly, replaced by questioning, uncomfortable glances from around the circle.

Ann felt mortified. She was embarrassed to death for Tara—and equally embarrassed to be seen with her. She wanted to just ignore her and pretend they weren't friends so the other kids wouldn't think she was rude too. But on the other hand, Tara was her guest.

---

## What would you do?

*If Ann tries to smooth over the situation, turn to page 23.*
*If she ignores Tara, turn to page 27.*

But she played along—refusing the wine cooler had been hard enough. Why risk offending Tara over some dumb movie that would go in her head, totally bypass her brain, then disappear forever?

Still, the feeling of revulsion grew in her—the heroine seemed to be fighting off either rape or mutilation in every scene, and blood spurted around like ketchup at a school picnic.

"Yuck," she groaned, finally jumping to her feet and turning her back to the screen. She walked to the double-glass doors of the den and looked at the paintings on the wall in the next room.

"What's wrong?" asked Tara. "Hey, are you sick?"

"I just can't get into this movie," she explained. "It's so ... gross. All that chopping."

Tara leaned forward and pressed a button to pause the action. Ann glanced at the heroine frozen in bloody torment on the screen and grimaced.

"You know, for people who don't have their head on straight, this kind of movie can make them confuse illusion and reality."

Tara turned off the set and came to stand beside Ann.

"Really?" she shrugged. "I never thought about it."

"And it's like rape is exciting, when it's really so pathetic," Ann went on. "I don't know. That probably doesn't make sense."

Tara stared at her shoes and didn't answer. Ann swallowed hard and decided to plunge in and say what was most on her mind.

"Tara? Listen, I like you. You're so funny and smart. I guess I'm just a little surprised that you're into this stuff. You just seem too ... good for it. Too smart. Or something."

Ann's neck was burning—she couldn't believe she'd said that. Now Tara would never want to see her again.

But suddenly, Tara was crying. Two slow tears hit the thick carpet by her Reeboks.

"You know, Ann, you remind me so much of Jillian," she whispered. "No one else has ever talked to me like that, scolded me and cared enough to try to get me to be stronger. I miss her so much!"

"Was Jillian a friend of yours back in Chicago?"

Tara shook her head miserably. "My sister. She was ... killed. By a drunk driver, six months ago."

Everything inside Ann froze with sympathy—and with fear.

She'd never been this close to grief before, and she didn't know what to do, how to respond or even what to say next. She suddenly felt uncomfortable with Tara, like Tara needed something from her Ann didn't know how to give. She wanted to get away, to go home.

## What would you do?

*If Ann reaches out to Tara, turn to page 106.*
*If she escapes instead as soon as she can, turn to page 85.*

"Uh, Tara? I forgot, I'm supposed to do a couple of loads of laundry this morning at home," she said in a rush, jumping to her feet .

"Oh, okay. Sure," Tara said, her eyes still on the screen. "See you at school then. Bye."

Ann could tell from Tara's tone that she recognized a lame excuse when she heard one and that her feelings were hurt. But then it was her own fault, wasn't it? Shouldn't she have realized Ann wasn't into this kind of movie either?

Regret and anger fought inside Ann. She really wanted Tara to think she'd be a good friend. On the other hand, she felt used—like Tara had tried to foist offensive stuff on her at every turn.

Why couldn't Tara have taken the time to get to know the real Ann, the one inside her that nobody much got a glimpse of?

But on the other hand, Ann realized her real self didn't exactly shine for the world to see. She was too shy and self-conscious for that to happen. Like everybody else, Tara just had to guess at what she was like and had guessed wrong.

■

The phone was ringing when Ann walked through the door at home, and she picked it up listlessly, sure it was for Mom.

But it was Rachelle Washington from youth group.

"Hi, Ann. I was just calling to see what you're doin' today."

Ann leaned against the phone table in the hall, glad to hear a friendly voice. This was incredible—two people had called for her in the same day. Rachelle had called a few times before, but Ann had never been able to think of much to say. Today, though, she had a hot topic still simmering in her head. All the kids would be super-interested in the stuff that had gone on at Tara's today. She was sure of that.

Of course, Tara might not be crazy about having the details of her lifestyle made public. But talking to the church kids about it surely wasn't gossiping, was it, since they'd only want to help?

## What would you do?

*If Ann tells Rachelle all about her morning with Tara, turn to page 95.*

*If she keeps it confidential, turn to page 104.*

Ann thought about mentioning her youth group meetings, where they talk about the false comfort of materialism and drinking and how following God brings true happiness. But she decided this wasn't the time or place for a big heavy discussion like that. If she wanted Tara's friendship, she sensed she needed to loosen up and just play along.

So for the rest of the afternoon, Ann walked with Tara from store to store, pretending to be cool and to admire all she saw.

"This stuff is so boring," Tara sighed, picking up a handful of gold chains from a display case at Dorflinger's and dropping them in a pile. "Same old styles, same old colors. I thought maybe there'd be something new and exciting out this spring, but I've got bunches of all this stuff already."

"Yeah, me too," Ann echoed, copying Tara's bored tone, mostly just to say something. Tara was doing all the talking.

"You do?" Tara asked, acting more interested. "You *do* have lots of clothes and jewelry, then, huh?"

Ann felt her neck burn, but it was too late to be honest now. "Sure," she said, then swallowed hard. "Well, I mean my mother is always bringing home stuff for me, even though my closet is practically ready to explode."

Ann fought the temptation to touch her nose, to see if it had grown from that lie. Not only could she and Mom not begin to afford to shop in stores like these, but they really had no desire to. Mom had always taught that enough was enough, and what Ann learned in church about Jesus' teachings reinforced that idea.

Still, Ann could see that her fib had definitely impressed Tara. Some people judged your worthiness by your possessions, and Tara seemed to be one of those people. So what was the harm?

"You know Ann, the more I get to know you the more I can see that you and I really have a lot in common." Tara smiled and tossed her hair over one shoulder. "I'm glad I called you."

"Me too." Ann tried not to listen to the little nagging voice inside her that warned that Tara didn't really know her and in fact was getting to know the real Ann less all the time.

"Listen, I have a great idea," Tara said, leaning toward Ann excitedly. "I keep a lot of my wardrobe and my best stereo system at our lake house. Why don't you come out with me next weekend, and I can show them to you? Oh, that would be so fun! You'll love our place—it's beautiful. And maybe it would even be warm enough for us to water-ski!"

The invitation was so tempting. Of course, Ann had obligations at church next weekend, including the program in youth group. And there was also that pesky nagging voice, asking if the real non-rich Ann would've received this invitation.

## What would you do?

*If Ann goes to the lake with Tara, turn to page 98.*
*If she stays home, turn to page 129.*

"Well, you know," Ann began slowly, "We do service projects and have Bible studies and stuff."

"Ha!" Tara exploded, nearly choking on her drink. She tossed her hair, laughing and shaking her head. "See, now that's why everybody knows that Christian stuff is a bust. Here you are relaxing and drinking a wine cooler, but I'll bet you wouldn't be caught dead drinking at one of your Bible studies!"

Ann felt stunned and too upset to respond. She was ashamed of the bottle in her hand—even though she hadn't drunk any—and wanted to smash it on the pool deck into a jillion pieces. But no amount of bottle smashing would undo the message she'd already sent.

After a few pensive moments, Ann tried to change the subject, but Tara kept coming back to the church issue.

Finally, Ann said abruptly, "Uh, listen Tara. I gotta go. I just remembered something I have to take care of this morning."

Without waiting for a response from Tara, she quickly walked through the side yard and didn't look back.

■

The next day in Sunday school, Ann was even quieter than usual, and finally Rachelle Washington whispered in her ear, "What's wrong? You feeling okay?"

Ann brusquely shook her head no. But at youth group that night, she'd brooded so long and hard about her Saturday morning at Tara's she felt like she was going to explode.

"I ... I've got something to ask you guys," she said quietly when the group was in a sharing circle. "Something strange happened to me yesterday. I met this girl, a non-Christian, and I sort of was getting ready to invite her to come with me to church when out of the blue she started talking about how fake Christians are."

Everybody was looking at her intensely.

"Out of the blue?" Jason Kyle asked gently.

Ann dropped her eyes and nodded, too ashamed to include the wine cooler in her story.

"They're the ones who're hypocritical!" Cora Bagis said, smacking her gum in a disgusted way. "Boy, it really burns me up when people put Christians down like that."

A few other kids nodded in agreement.

"I don't even try to reason with people like that," Cora added, twirling a lock of her dark, wavy hair. "The best policy is not to argue with them. They won't listen to reason, so I just walk away and leave 'em to God."

Chris Peters, the youth minister, put his chin in his hands and scrunched his forehead in thought.

"I don't know," he said. "I mean, you say leave it to God. But maybe God is leaving it to us, you know?"

"I don't know," Jason said. "It's not that easy. I mean, how do you reach out when someone rejects you like that?"

An idea was blooming in Ann's head—why couldn't they have a series of meetings about just that, making a plan for reaching out to non-Christians? She struggled to get up her nerve to suggest that, to fight past the shyness that had always kept her from offering her ideas in youth group.

---

## What would you do?

*If Ann suggests studying this topic, turn to page 66.*
*If she decides not to bring it up, turn to page 71.*

Ann ate a quick slice of pizza then went for a walk to think.
Maybe she *was* feeling a little sorry for herself. What would she
really be risking if she took Mom's advice and invited some girls
for a sleepover? They might make up some transparent excuses
for why they couldn't come. That would hurt, but probably no
worse than she hurt right now.

By the time Ann got back to the house, she'd made her decision. "Mom, I'm going to have a party. Will you help?"

"Of course, Annie." Mom gave her a quick, supportive hug.
"Why don't you start planning right now? I think you'll be surprised how much fun it'll be."

"You can?" She knew she sounded a little weird, acting
surprised like this every time someone said yes to her invitation.
But, well, she *was* surprised. "Great, Ginger! See you at 7 next
Friday night, then!"

"Knock, knock." Mom stood smiling in the doorway as Ann
hung up the phone. "I take it from the expression on your face
that your party is coming together?"

"Oh, Mom, I can't believe this! I've called, let's see, eight
people. And six are coming! The other two said they wished they
could, but they were going to Hillary Stanton's birthday party next
Friday night. This is so cool!"

Her mother laughed and crossed the room to give her a
quick hug. "Just let me know if you need my help, okay?"

"Thanks," Ann said automatically, her head buzzing with
plans. Then she looked up. "Mom? Really, thanks."

Ann was nervous the whole week before the party, especially
Friday afternoon as she checked and rechecked her food supplies
and made triple sure she'd remembered to rent movies. She tried
not to panic when her mind touched the possibility that
everybody would be bored at her party.

But that didn't happen. From the minute the six other girls
arrived, there was so much silliness and goofing around that Ann
couldn't even find time to start any of the three movies. Her
earlier nervousness seemed silly to her now—just being together
was what was making the party fun.

At a certain point in the evening, the talk began to center on the other party in town that night—Hillary Stanton's.

"I guess most of the popular kids are there." Cora Bagis threw a piece of caramel corn into the air and caught it in her mouth. "I bet they're all comparing fakey smiles."

"Well, it's true that Hillary and her friends are a bunch of snobs," Ginger Edwards said with a shrug. "If the world was ending at noon, they'd walk all over each other to get control of the nearest mirror so they could go out in style."

Stacy Powell, giggling, threw a pillow toward Ginger, lost her balance and somersaulted off the bed. "You know what we ought to do? We ought to go over there and crash their party!"

"Yeah!" Janene Grant shouted from where she was sitting cross-legged on Ann's vanity table. "We could sneak around under the windows and find out what they look like without the tons of makeup they wear. We could even make scary noises so they'd think Hillary's house is haunted!"

She did a gruesome Boris Karloff imitation, and everybody rolled around howling with laughter at their silly plans.

Ann couldn't be sure if they were serious about any of this, but it was making her uneasy. For one thing, she didn't like gossiping, and Hillary and her gang seemed okay. Not the most friendly kids in school, maybe a bit stuck-up. But basically okay.

"Listen you guys, I rented these neat movies ..." she began, hoping to put the party on a different track.

"Time for movies later, Ann," Cora said, jumping to her feet. "Okay, who's coming to Hillary's?"

"But what'll we do there?" Janene asked. "Seriously. What?"

Cora, grinning slyly, slipped dramatically into the bathroom adjoining Ann's room and was back in a flash.

"Voilà!" She produced two rolls of toilet paper from behind her back. "We'll get some more of this stuff from the 7-11 down the block and T.P. her yard."

Again, all the girls bent double with giggles, then started hunting for their shoes and jackets.

## What would you do?

*If Ann goes along to T.P. Hillary's house, turn to page 70.*
*If she stays behind while the others go, turn to page 47.*

"Well, excuse us, Miss Chicago!" Ann said with a grin, hoping Tara could take a little teasing.

A few of the kids smiled and nodded, and a couple even chuckled. The tension broke—a little at least—and Ann breathed a mental sigh of relief.

Then Tom Kemper, the group president, who was one of the people who'd chuckled, stood up. He was tall and thin, and his bright-red suspenders made him look like a rocket ready to be launched. "Yes, we spent days and days stitching these carpet squares together," he said, holding an imaginary microphone to his mouth. "Notice the fine craftsmanship—these neat stitches and the perfect straightness of each seam."

As Tom pointed out one particularly sloppy carpet section that bore a liberal helping of dried-in nacho cheese sauce, several kids laughed or made sarcastic faces.

Tara had been frowning in confusion, but now broke down in good-natured giggles herself. "Okay, okay. Sorry I mentioned it!"

"By the way, everybody," Ann said when things had settled. "I'd like to introduce you to Tara Hastings. She's new."

Everybody around the circle said in well-practiced unison, "Hi, Tara," then everybody expanded to give Tara and Ann room to sit down.

■

After the meeting, Ann and Tara said their goodbyes to the group, then took off in the old Volkswagen Rabbit Ann got to drive when Mom was home from work.

"Thanks for inviting me tonight," Tara said on the way home. "You know, though, I just didn't feel like I fit in. There's something about church kids I can't explain."

Ann took a deep breath and let it out. Here it came—the ridicule she'd braced for all through the meeting, ever since their humiliating entrance. "What do you mean?" she asked sheepishly.

"I just ... I just feel awkward, like they're looking down on me or something." The words fumbled out of Tara's mouth. She cleared her throat. "That's why I came on so strong when we arrived—just nerves. Sorry I was such a jerk."

"Hey, no big deal." Ann's words masked her surprise at Tara's attitude. And all this time Ann had been afraid that Tara was looking down on them!

At home that night, Ann remembered the youth group had a couple of activities coming up and decided to call and invite Tara to one of them. She thought maybe Tara needed another chance to be around the kids in a fun, easy-going setting.

Would it be better to invite her to their monthly pizza-making bonanza in the church kitchen? Or after what Tara said about "church" kids, would it be better to invite her to the movie party the group had planned at Crestview Cinema—and steer clear of church turf altogether?

## What would you do?

*If Ann asks Tara to a pizza party with the group, turn to page 74.*
*If she asks her to a movie with friends from church, turn to page 79.*

As they neared Chastleman's Clothing Shoppe, Tara grabbed Ann by the elbow and pulled her toward the door.

"Come on, that old jean jacket you're wearing is ratty," she said bluntly. "Let's try some leather and suede on you."

Ann froze at the threshold of the store.

"Come on!" Tara demanded, but still Ann didn't budge.

"Uh, Tara? I don't think I can go in there and try things on that I wouldn't really, well, want. You know what I mean?"

Ann could tell from Tara's expression that she didn't know. She had no idea what Ann was talking about.

"See, well, I mean ... I'm just not interested in that kind of stuff. Anyway, uh, aren't you hungry?"

Ann could hardly breathe, she was so flustered. But to her huge relief, Tara sighed and shrugged.

"I guess I could eat, yeah."

■

"I can't believe this weird anti-clothes philosophy of yours. Were you born with it, or is it some kind of dread disease you caught?" Tara asked, taking a crunch of her taco and washing it down with Coke. "Seriously, Ann, it's pretty silly."

Ann forced a smile and took a long drink of cherry Coke before answering. "Get me through this, God," she thought, remembering the words on the little sticker from this morning.

"Well, it's not that I don't like neat clothes," she began. "It's just that in church and youth group I've learned not to want ... oh, I don't know ... I guess having super-nice stuff isn't all that important to me. There's more to life than what you wear."

She took another long drink to hide her nervousness and waited for Tara to respond to that.

"So, what else do you do in this youth group of yours?" Tara asked, expressionless.

Ann couldn't tell if that was a real question, or just a semi-sarcastic comment. Should she answer or just let it pass?

## What would you do?

*If Ann tells Tara more about her beliefs, turn to page 12.*
*If she's afraid to and changes the subject, turn to page 17.*

"You just don't understand," Ann choked out angrily. "I'm not like you, Mom, so just stay out of it, okay?"

She ran to her room, plopped on her bed and pulled herself into a tight ball. A little sliver of sunlight spilled through the drawn curtains, cutting across her bed. She got up and pulled the curtains tightly closed, then balled up again on her mattress, clutching a pillow. She wanted to stay hidden in darkness.

And at the same time, she hoped someone would find a way to reach in and pull her out into the light.

■

A couple of weeks later, Rachelle Washington sat beside Ann in church.

"Can you come over for a while this afternoon?" she whispered. "We could make posters for the youth group chili supper next month."

Ann wondered—was the invitation genuine or some kind of sympathy mission? Rachelle's mom and Ann's were good buddies—had they been talking? What if Mom had urged Rachelle's mother to urge Rachelle to reach out to Ann? How humiliating!

On the other hand, just possibly the invitation was genuine.

## What would you do?

*If Ann goes to Rachelle's, turn to page 38.*
*If she distrusts Rachelle's invitation and turns it down, turn to page 42.*

Ann flopped down cross-legged on the floor without a word to anybody, and after a few seconds, Tara sat down beside her. Ann edged away slightly. She knew the kids were expecting at least an introduction to Tara, but she couldn't talk past the throbbing lump of humiliation in her throat. Finally, Tara introduced herself, and the other kids responded politely enough.

To Ann, the meeting seemed to last a decade instead of just an hour. And when it was finally over and she drove Tara home, Ann still couldn't think of a thing to say to her.

"Thanks, Ann, for inviting me tonight," Tara said softly as they started up her driveway. "That wasn't too bad, for a church thing. I mean, there's bound to be some boredom, right? When's the next meeting? Same time next week? Can you pick me up again?"

Ann was too surprised to respond. Why in the world would Tara want to go again? Hadn't she felt how out of place she was, how tense the whole situation had been?

"I'm ... uh, not sure," Ann hedged. "We may not be meeting next week. I'll ... find out, or something."

Tara nodded and got out of the car. Ann watched as she walked, alone, toward her beautiful but dark house. It almost looked like she was dreading going inside. But how could that be? She had everything in there.

Everything but human companionship, said a tiny voice deep inside Ann. And something caught in her throat.

She needed to talk to somebody about Tara, and suddenly she knew just the person.

Reverend Sumner would probably still be at the church locking everything up after evening services. If she hurried, she could probably catch him.

■

"Okay, here I go. Got a tight hold, Ann?"

"Yeah, got it." She gripped the ladder securely as Reverend Sumner climbed, then balanced on the top rung to push a couple of thumbtacks into the banner they were hanging. Ann felt a sense of peace as they worked together. It had been good to talk about Tara with Reverend Sumner—to express what she was going through. He was so accepting of Ann's feelings.

"Boy, am I glad you happened by tonight!" He smiled down at her through the circle of his arms. "I guess I probably would've tried doing this all by myself. Might've broken my neck in the process." He stepped down a couple of rungs, then jumped to the floor, rubbing his hands in satisfaction. "Looks good, doesn't it? It should brighten up the fellowship hall a little."

She surveyed the big rainbow-color banner with its bold purple words and nodded agreement.

"I like the words. That verse. It's one of my favorites."

"Oh, it is?" Reverend Sumner raised his eyebrows and began to read. " 'Love one another as I have loved most of you.' That's a good verse, all right."

"You're kidding, right?" Ann cleared her throat. "There's not a 'most' in that verse, is there? It would change the whole meaning."

She glanced over at him. Sure enough, his gentle eyes were full of sly laughter behind his wire-rimmed glasses.

"Ann, I've been thinking about this friend you told me about. Sometimes it's hard to open a door to someone and keep it open. But if the verse on this banner had that 'most' in it, our whole faith would be changed and drastically diminished. Do you get what I mean? The message of Jesus Christ is a message of constant reaching out, not just to people we're sure of and feel good around all the time. But to everyone we come in contact with. "

"The youth group has a couple of big activities coming up this month. Why not invite your friend to one of them? Maybe it'll be easier to loosen up and break a little ice over food. Always works for me."

He patted his slight paunch, and he and Ann both laughed.

Ann's laughter was partly because of relief. His idea sounded just right to her, like something she could handle.

Now the only question was whether to invite Tara to the pizza-making party in the church kitchen or to let her get to know the kids on more neutral territory by inviting her to the movie party the youth group had planned at Crestview Cinema.

## What would you do?

*If Ann asks Tara to a pizza party with the group, turn to page 74.*
*If she asks her to the movie party, turn to page 79.*

Still, Ann just couldn't see herself taking a drink, even this one time. Besides, it would give Tara the wrong idea.

"I thought you meant ... a Coke," she murmured. "I mean, I'm sorry but, uh, I don't ... drink."

Tara shrugged. "No problem. I'll get you a Coke." She went back into the kitchen.

Ann was left wondering—had she blown it completely now? Tara had been polite and nonchalant about the cooler, but now did she really think Ann was a total no-fun-allowed prude, and would she get rid of her as quickly as she could?

But a couple of minutes later, Tara appeared in the kitchen doorway and called out to her.

"I've got a great idea! My parents have a new stereo television, and I just remembered I checked out some videos last night. Let's watch one before we study, okay?"

"Great!" Ann eagerly agreed.

As they microwaved popcorn, they talked about how it felt to move to a new school during junior year.

"All in all, it's a little worse than being hung by your thumbs," Tara concluded firmly, after a hilarious deadpan monologue of her first week's mishaps.

Ann giggled. "Yeah, it feels sort of rotten to start over all right. At least I moved early in the year. It must be really rough for you, so near the end of school."

"That's why I was so relieved when you agreed to come over today. You're the first friend I've made here."

Ann felt herself glow all over at those words. They took the popcorn into the den, still chatting furiously. But when the movie started, Tara put her finger to her lips.

"Okay, no more talking," she whispered. "I just love this kind of movie, but it spoils the suspense if you talk through it."

Ann nodded, and happily leaned back against the sofa pillows to enjoy the flick. But within minutes, she felt rigid with disgust and almost nauseous. She had no taste for R-rated horror movies like the one they were watching.

"Wow, did you see that? Gross!" Tara breathed after the third or fourth gruesome death scene. "How do they make that look so real?"

Ann felt miserably uncomfortable. It made her sick to think that the morning—which had been going so well—was now reduced to this kind of perverted "entertainment." She wondered if she should make some excuse and leave.

## What would you do?

*If Ann decides to leave, turn to page 16.*
*If she stays and watches the movie, turn to page 14.*

Ann plastered a bright smile on her face and raised her hand in an exuberant wave, hoping she was reading the situation wrong. Maybe Tara would just wave back and everything would be cool.

But Tara abruptly turned her back on Ann and slammed her locker shut. Ann reluctantly hurried over to her.

"Tara, I . . . I'm sorry. I . . ."

"I liked you, Ann," Tara broke in, whirling back around with tears in her eyes. "How could you have talked about me to everybody like that? How could you?"

Shame made Ann's neck burn. "Can we go somewhere and talk, Tara?" she forced out. "Outside? We could sit on the steps by the gym."

Tara stared stonily at her, and Ann knew she was going to just walk away. But Tara spoke instead, her voice trembling a little with hurt and anger.

"Let's go, then. I want to hear your explanation."

■

"I know this doesn't excuse what I did but . . . but I felt really insecure when you invited me over the other day," Ann began. She picked up a rock and squeezed it nervously. "See, I'm really self-conscious. And, well, I'm not into the kinds of things you are, but I was too . . . too scared to say anything to you. Like the wine cooler. And that movie. They both made me nervous."

"Then why didn't you just say so?" Tara asked.

"I told you—I was too scared."

"But not too scared to blab about my personal life all over the school!"

"Yes," Ann whispered. "I'm sorry. I just . . . blew it, I guess. I feel really rotten about it." Ann looked at Tara timidly. "Really."

Tara didn't answer for a while. She stared across the Crestview High campus, frowning in thought, and finally spoke without looking directly at Ann.

"You really hurt me, Ann. But I guess everybody makes mistakes. Heck, I've blown it a couple of times myself." Tara smiled, looking at Ann. "But if you're not into drinking or scary movies, what are you into? I mean, I'm up for other things."

Ann felt lightheaded with relief. "Thanks, Tara. For giving me another chance, I mean. And I've got a great idea. There's this movie party the youth group at our church is sponsoring next week. Come with me. When the other kids see how you really are, maybe it'll undo the damage I've done."

Tara looked her in the eye, smiled slightly, and shrugged.

"Okay," she said. "Sure, I'd like to come."

∎

At the movie party, Tara fit in great with the other kids. Too great, in fact. Though Tara couldn't have known it, Ann had harbored a crush for ages on Jason Kyle. And, in fact, she even thought Jason might possibly think she was all right too. But Jason got one good look at Tara and began flirting with her. And Tara flirted right back.

Well, what did Ann expect? Tara was great-looking and a lot of fun, and so was Jason. In fact, anybody with eyes could see they made a really attractive couple.

Still ...

When the group went for tacos after the movie, Jason grabbed an empty chair from right beside Ann and shoved it into a skinny space next to Tara.

Ann felt her eyes burn, and her stomach tied itself into a tight knot. Enough was enough!

## What would you do?

*If Ann angrily confronts Tara about Jason, turn to page 56.*
*If Ann is hurt and snubs Tara from then on, turn to page 65.*

Ann didn't exactly mean to brood after Janene left, but it was an easy thing to fall into. Yes, it was much easier to spend her time lying on her bed, thinking of the good times while comforting tears overtook her than it would've been to get up the courage to talk to new people, or to have another party or something like that.

She drifted, telling herself that one of these days she'd maybe try to reach out to some other kids. But not today. And probably not tomorrow either.

She was still too sad. In the cafeteria, she ate with her eyes down, looking at no one. In the halls, she pretended to read over her homework so she wouldn't meet anyone's gaze.

And at home, there were her room, her bed, her good memories and the comforting tears of nostalgia they brought.

A few weeks passed, then one day Ann was reading—by herself of course—in the school library when Desiree Snyder unexpectedly sat down across from her. With one bright purple nail, Desiree reached out and boldly lowered Ann's book.

"Do you plan to squander your vital energy like this forever?" Desiree asked point-blank. "There are bad vibrations coming from you, Ann Tyler. Very bad vibrations."

Ann gulped, totally off-balance. Desiree and her crowd were the "artsy" kids at Crestview High, and all the other kids treated them with a combination of fear and grudging respect. Everyone knew they were into some weird things, with their New-Age ideas and their mysterious parties in apartments near the college campus. But they were fascinating too. Desiree's hair was black, cropped very short, and she dressed all in black except for bright bangle jewelry. She was so strikingly pale Ann thought she must use baby powder or something to get that effect.

"I'm ... I'm okay," Ann forced out.

Desiree sighed. "I won't argue with you, but I'll tell you this—I can help you. We can help you. You should come to our meeting—tonight."

She left a slip of paper on the table in front of Ann, and slipped away like a puff of smoke.

■

Ann didn't seriously think about going to the meeting 'til that night. Alone in her room, she found it hard to slip into her old habit of comfortable brooding. The idea of the meeting kept

getting in the way. Well, what did she have to lose?

The address Desiree had given her was for a place only a few miles away. She slipped out and found it with no trouble.

She timidly knocked on the door at 501 Hamilton. It was opened by a college boy with a ponytail and one dangling earring who silently led her into a room where a couple of dozen kids were seated on pillows around a cluster of burning white candles. No one acknowledged the interruption when she squeezed in between two kids she knew a little from school.

"Creation without imagination is nothing, worthless, worse than worthless. Pathetic," pronounced a young woman with black-lined eyes that looked huge in the candlelight.

Several others murmured and raised glasses in agreement. Ann then noticed wine glasses on the floor by most of the people. And something else, marijuana smoke, hung over the circle.

Her eyes adjusted to the dim light, and then she noticed the weed being passed from person to person along the opposite side of the circle.

"We have to constantly see and evaluate life with the clear, unclouded eyes of a child." This comment came from Desiree, and drew solemn nods of agreement. Ann looked toward Desiree and saw that the circling marijuana was now clasped between her thumb and forefinger. She took a long hit, held it, let it out and spoke again, a little huskily. "Philosophers, such as Jesus Christ, have long known this to be true. That's why Christ said that the kingdom of heaven belonged to children. The kingdom of heaven isn't some mythic place in the clouds, but is right here on Earth, for anyone with imagination enough to see it."

Everything was suddenly heady and a little frightening to Ann—both the ideas and the marijuana smoke. She began to feel something like a spell falling over her, and wondered whether to resist or let it happen.

## What would you do?

*If she resists the ideas, turn to page 119.*
*If she lets them sweep over her, turn to page 81.*

Ann's head spun with "if onlys." If only she'd reached out to Tara and given her the friendship she craved. If only she'd pushed past her own self-centeredness to give a little more and understand a little more of what was going on in Tara's life.

"Honey, I know you're sad about Tara. That's only natural," Mom said gently at dinner one night a couple of weeks after Tara's death. "But you're letting yourself brood and become morbid about this. You need to get out of your room, to get your mind on something else."

Ann pushed her peas around and didn't answer. How could she tell Mom, or anyone, that it was guilt not sadness that made her feel that she herself was drowning? In fact, that guilt was even finding its way into her dreams. Most nights she woke shivering after dreaming that she was in Tara's pool, trying to fight her way to the surface but trapped helplessly beneath tons of water.

She lost weight, and dark circles etched themselves beneath her eyes. Maybe the worst part was that she couldn't find the comfort and guidance she'd always found in her church connections. She couldn't possibly tell Reverend Sumner that she'd done such an awful thing and treated Tara as she had. The kids in youth group would surely hate her if she confessed to them.

And she couldn't even pray about it. She knew God was love, so how could he understand an act as unloving as the way she'd turned her back on Tara?

It began to really bother her even being in the church building, where every symbol reminded her of the kind of unselfish love she'd proven herself to be tragically incapable of giving. So she quit attending. The first two Sundays she missed, she pleaded a stomachache. But the third, Mom didn't buy that.

"Annie." She sat on the edge of Ann's bed and took both her hands. "I thought this grief of yours would pass, but instead it's become a very serious problem. I'm making an appointment at the counseling center for you to talk to someone."

"It won't do any good, Mom," she said listlessly. But she lacked the energy to argue, and the next day she went along reluctantly to Dr. Karrick's office.

■

For the first few sessions, Ann let Dr. Karrick ask questions, and kept her own emotions and thoughts carefully sealed up. But then one day, Dr. Karrick said that awful, magic word—guilt—that cut through the carefully constructed box Ann was living in.

"Every suicide leaves behind guilt in those close to that person. Ann, I believe, for whatever reasons, you're feeling guilt about Tara, destructive guilt that's eating you alive."

That's when the tears started—tears Ann thought would never stop.

"Ann, now listen to me," Dr. Karrick said firmly as Ann sobbed with her face in her own hands. "Suicide is an individual decision. You didn't make that decision. Tara did. Period. All of us do things we later wish we'd done differently. Regret is a part of life for everybody. But guilt is a destructive, paralyzing emotion, and you've got to work on ridding yourself of it. Ann, let the guilt go."

Easier said than done. Still, Ann felt immense relief just having things out in the open. In fact, one afternoon she went into the sanctuary at church and sat there alone. It took her a long time to get up the courage to face the cross that hung over the altar. And it took her even longer to get past the burning lump in her chest and to ask God what she had to know.

"Can you ... forgive me, Lord?"

She'd no sooner said the words than she knew she was already forgiven. She even suddenly understood that the people she loved at church would support her as she slowly healed. She felt sure about that now, and it gave her the strength to learn from what had happened and to live again.

■

Ann's senior year, a family moved next door who'd never been to church. They had a girl Ann's age, Cyllia, who was withdrawn and moody, but Ann persisted in trying to be friends with her and finally interested her in church and youth group.

It was hard for Ann, self-conscious as she was, to reach out that much. It would've been easy at many points to back away. But this time, she went the second mile.

The End

" ... seven, eight, nine. Done! Nine posters, and all of them too cool for words."

Ann laughed at Rachelle's description of their handiwork and helped her gather up the markers from the floor of her bedroom.

"Rachelle, thanks for inviting me over, even if it was your mother's idea or something."

"Huh? My mother's idea? What are you talking about? Ann, I've invited you before, remember? I'm glad you finally squeezed me into your frantic schedule."

They both smiled at that, and Ann shrugged. "Yeah, I guess I tend to stick pretty close to home on weekends. I'm sort of shy, in case you haven't noticed."

"Well, join the club," Rachelle said. "You're not the only shy woman in this town."

"Oh come on, not you!" Ann immediately denied. "You've got gobs of friends!"

Rachelle put down her posters and gave Ann a serious look.

"I've got this trick I pull on myself. I just make a part of my mind click off when I meet someone new," she said thoughtfully. "There's always a little voice in my head that tells me 'You're too shy! They won't like you. You won't know what to say!' But I've learned to shush that voice and to tell myself instead that there are plenty of good things about me. In fact, sometimes I even mentally run through those good things before I go up to someone to talk to them."

The phone on her dresser suddenly rang, breaking off their conversation. Ann was left thinking about what Rachelle had said. Why couldn't that system work for her too?

"It's some kids from school," Rachelle whispered after a couple of minutes of phone conversation. "They want us to come to a party this afternoon. At Jamie White's house."

"Us?" Ann asked, knowing the invitation had only been for Rachelle.

Rachelle uncovered the receiver, and told Jamie they'd be there in a few minutes. She raised her eyebrows toward Ann for confirmation, and Ann nodded timidly.

"Thanks," Ann said when Rachelle hung up the phone. "For including me, I mean."

"Jamie only lives a few blocks from you, Ann, so you can go home whenever you want, okay? And remember—think those good thoughts about yourself."

"Okay, I'll try," Ann laughed.

■

When Rachelle parked at Jamie's curb, pounding music from inside the house reached out and surrounded the car.

"Get in here!" Jamie himself and a couple of other guys yelled from the front porch. They all three had beers in their hands, and Jamie was smoking.

"All right!" Joe Armando called over Jamie's shoulder. "Mas chicas finas!"

A couple of girls, overhearing, came out of the house and jumped on Joe from behind, tickling him and yelling that he was a male-chauvinist pig and they were going to teach him a lesson.

"All right!" he yelled happily as they drug him back into the house. "I like it! I like it!"

"Well," Rachelle said, taking a deep breath and opening her car door. "Ready for this?"

It was dark in the house—all the curtains were pulled, and there was lots of smoke. You could tell immediately there were no adults anywhere around—too many couples openly necking for that. One corner held a big cooler of beer, another was filled with a stereo system that throbbed out walls of sound.

James Harper came over, put his arm around Rachelle's shoulders and led her away. She looked back at Ann and shot her a "sorry but I'll see you later" smile. A few seconds later, Peter Thompson came up and leaned against the part of the wall where Ann was trying to dissolve into the woodwork. He bent close to her, winked and held up his beer.

"Want one?" he mouthed.

Drinking was the last thing on Ann's mind, but she didn't know what to do. Even though she never drank, maybe she should just hold one, so she wouldn't feel so conspicuous. Or maybe she should just get out of here and not worry about explanations.

## What would you do?

*If Ann decides to make an escape, go to page 112.*
*If she stays awhile, go to page 53.*

"No!" she told herself firmly. "I just can't face being around Tara! I wouldn't know what to say, or do, or . . . or anything!"

Then, with the pillow still bundled tightly around her head, she let everything out in a long, hot cry.

■

She pulled herself together an hour or so later, and spent the morning and early afternoon thoroughly cleaning the house. She did that every Saturday, and she knew Mom appreciated it.

Still, there was that same look of concern in Mom's eyes when she arrived home that afternoon that there had been at breakfast. She handed Ann the pizza she'd brought with a cheerful flourish and tried to act casual as she laid down her purse and remarked about the beautiful weather. But the look was there. The concern was in her eyes.

"We were really busy at the library this morning, especially after story hour. I guess teachers are assigning lots of book reports this month. How has your day been so far, honey?"

"Okay," said Ann, getting place mats from the drawer, avoiding Mom's eyes.

Mom cleared her throat. "The house looks great, Annie. But I told you that I'd take care of it, didn't I? You could've just had some fun today."

Before she knew what was happening, the tears from this morning were back in full force, throbbing in Ann's throat. The paper napkins she was folding blurred, and she knew if she tried to talk she wouldn't be able to.

"Oh, honey," Mom said softly, coming up behind her to take her shoulders in her hands. "I know how you're feeling. I really do. There's nothing harder in the world than making and keeping good friends, especially at your age."

"How can you possibly know anything about that?" Ann sobbed. "You can talk to people so easily, and I know you were popular in school. So you can't know what it's like to feel like people are making fun of you and laughing behind your back. To feel tongue-tied, and afraid and flustered all the time. Nobody wants to be with me, and it hurts! It hurts, Mom!"

"But Annie, people *do* want to be with you!" Mom's voice was gentle but persistent. "What about those girls from youth group? They've called you several times, but you brush them off. I know you don't know you're doing it, but you send signals that say you're not interested in their friendship. Do you think you're the only one capable of feeling rejected? They feel rejected, too, when you do that, honey."

"But I'm afraid, Mom! What will I talk about to them? What will we do that I'm good at?"

Ann was shredding a soggy napkin, and Mom reached down and touched her hand. "Annie, you just said that I was popular in school, but that's not exactly right. I had friends, yes, but it was terrifying for me at first making them. I was at least as shy as you are at your age, and I didn't have the advantage of a great sense of humor like you have. I think most so-called popular people have their share of insecurities too."

"Yeah, right." Ann began, rolling her eyes.

"Let me finish," Mom commanded quietly. "When I was 15, I finally forced myself to have a party, to actually get on the phone and invite some people over. I was positive it would be a disaster. It was agony, planning it, waiting. But you know what? It wasn't a disaster. It was fun. And something one of the girls who came said has stuck with me all these years. She said people thought I was stuck-up since I kept to myself all the time, and they were surprised and flattered that I'd finally invited them over. I was shocked! Me, stuck-up? But Annie, people can't read your mind. They think funny things sometimes when you don't reach out."

"Nobody thinks I'm stuck-up, Mom. Nobody thinks about me period, or wants to. I'm just a ... a nobody."

"Now you're feeling sorry for yourself, Annie," Mom said firmly. "And I hate to hear you fall into that."

Ann wondered—was she feeling sorry for herself? Or did Mom just fail to understand what was going on inside her?

## What would you do?

*If Ann decides Mom is right, turn to page 21.*
*If she thinks Mom really doesn't understand, turn to page 26.*

Ann decided not to take a chance.

"Thanks anyway, but I've got stuff to do this afternoon," she said quickly, forcing a tight smile.

"Oh, okay." Rachelle smiled back, but she got up and moved to the pew where most of the other senior highers were sitting, leaving Ann alone. A heaviness settled inside Ann, and it was a strain to concentrate on the service. The organ music, the hymns, even the prayers—everything ran together in a sad blur.

The sadness didn't go away that day, or the next. But after a while, Ann developed a way of shutting it out. She built a wall around her feelings and gradually decided she didn't need other people to be content. She sat apart at youth group meetings and always chose the desk in the far back corner at school. She avoided clubs and developed some solitary skills, like playing the violin and drawing.

She was content. Her life was controlled, without highs or lows. Being around people seemed more and more dangerous to her. Emotional involvement was too much of a risk.

After college, she got a job as a copy editor at a small magazine. She had a cubbyhole office to herself and didn't associate much with her co-workers. At home, she had two cats for company. At Christmas her mother usually came to visit.

But after her mom died, Ann quit getting a tree at Christmas.

After all, the cats just spread the needles all over the floor. And there really wasn't anyone she wanted to buy a present for. So she just didn't bother with those meaningless frills.

Instead, every Christmas Eve, Ann would buy a bottle of cheap wine, sit on her sofa and watch *It's a Wonderful Life*.

And drink herself to sleep.

The End

"Come on, Ann. Other kids will come and be with us if they want to be," Cora urged. "I mean, it's not like we have this classroom or the youth room locked and bolted or anything."

"Yeah, and aren't we good enough for you, just the way we are?" Jason ran his hands through his hair and straightened his tie in a crazy, mock-sophisticated way.

Everybody laughed then, and with a slight sigh that nobody caught, Mrs. Rossmond began the lesson.

But still, Ann was troubled. Maybe if the group wasn't going to reach out to anyone new, it was time to strike out on her own. Maybe she could just go slow with Tara. She decided not to intimidate her by inviting her to church yet but to just be a friend to her in other ways and see what developed.

The next Saturday, she got up the nerve to call Tara. Tara was delighted to hear from her, and they started doing some things together.

One morning they were watching a movie on Tara's VCR, when Ann brought up something that still puzzled her.

"Tara, when you first invited me over, you said it was because you needed help studying, but you didn't really plan for us to study that day, did you?"

Tara shrugged. "Can't remember."

"Well, I'm just curious. Did you have some other reason for, uh, choosing me, of all people, to invite? I mean I'm not exactly the flashiest person in the junior class! I'm surprised you'd even ... notice me at all."

"Oh, I noticed you," Tara said, her voice low and suddenly shaky. "I noticed you right away. You look a little like, uh, Jillian. You act a lot like her too. She was quiet. A good listener."

Ann was surprised to see that Tara was quietly crying.

"Was Jillian a friend of yours back in Chicago?"

Tara shook her head, biting her lip. "My sister. She was ... killed. By a drunk driver six months ago."

Ann was stunned—she'd never been this close to grief before, and she didn't know how to react. She knew she should offer some kind of comfort to Tara, but she didn't know how to begin.

## What would you do?

*If Ann reaches out to Tara, turn to page 106.*
*If she feels too awkward to help, turn to page 85.*

And besides, Ann liked the adventure of this. And she'd liked Tim's arms, strong around her when they'd danced. She was sure she could keep their relationship tonight on a far-less-advanced level than Tara and Roger's.

And she did. She and Tim were just listening to music and cuddling when Tara and Roger stumbled out of their bedroom at 2 a.m., smiling sheepishly.

Everything had worked out fine, or so Ann thought as she and Tara drove home through the warm May sunshine that early Sunday evening. Their friendship cooled a lot after that, but only because Tara and Roger had become inseparable. Tara didn't have time for anyone else, even Ann.

And Ann missed Tara—a lot. Partly because now she found herself craving the kind of excitement and danger she'd felt that night at the lake. Without Tara and her cabin, life seemed so dull and boring she sometimes thought she'd scream.

And then one night early in September, Ann came in from raking the lawn to find Mom white-faced, gripping the phone and listening to someone on the other end angry enough to be heard across the room.

It sounded like Tara's mother. Ann's stomach clenched.

"Oh, Ann," Mom whispered, putting a hand to her mouth when she'd hung up the phone. "Tara is pregnant. She's on her way right now to a boarding school in Europe. Her mother thinks it happened ..." She tried to keep her voice from shaking. "She thinks it happened that night you girls were at the lake. But it couldn't have ... could it?"

Ann felt like the air had been sucked out of her. Her ears began ringing.

"Ann?" Mom's voice was tight now. "Could it have?"

"How should I know?" Ann exploded. "Since when am I Tara's guardian?"

"Then Roger *was* at the lake that night," Mom said. "And were there other boys there, Ann?"

"Why are you giving me the third degree like this?" she screamed and slammed out the back door.

Mom followed.

"Because, young lady, a good friend of yours is now in deep trouble, and I want to know if you had some responsibility for getting her there!"

Ann had never heard Mom so upset. Ann whirled around toward her mother, anger and shame fighting inside her. Of course she felt guilty about Tara. But what could she have done? Tara had made up her own mind, right?

"Mom, just back off, okay? You're suffocating me." Ann's teeth were clenched.

"Ann, I won't be talked to like that. You're grounded."

■

The next week, Desiree Snyder, one of Tara's chums, invited Ann to attend a meeting of an "artsy" club some of the more sophisticated kids at school belonged to.

"We talk about New-Age ideas, the history of philosophy, fascinating stuff like that," Desiree explained, tapping the cafeteria table with her long purple nails. "I think you'd like Philosophy Club, and I think you'd like us."

"I can't go anywhere," Ann said listlessly. "I'm grounded."

"Then sneak out, of course." Desiree shrugged and yawned. "Or are you saying your Mommy owns you?"

Desiree got up and walked away, leaving the address of the meeting on the table in front of Ann. Ann watched her leave—her pale skin looked striking against her short black hair and black shirt. Like most kids at Crestview High, Ann had always been a little intimidated by Desiree's far-out group. But now, Ann thought they just might be the answer to the craving for adventure building in her. And besides, she felt flattered that Desiree had singled her out to invite to this club, whatever it was.

She took Desiree's advice, and the night of the meeting, she sneaked out her bedroom window.

When she knocked at the door of 501 Hamilton, an apartment near the college campus, it was opened by a boy with a ponytail and one dangling earring who wordlessly led her into a room where a couple of dozen kids were seated on pillows around a cluster of burning white candles.

There was a discussion going on, something about imagination. As Ann's eyes became accustomed to the dim light, she recognized several kids from Desiree's crowd. The others looked older, like college students. Some of the people held wine glasses. A haze of sweet-smelling smoke hung over the circle.

She quietly sat down on a pillow and listened for a while.

After she'd been there about half an hour, a thin young man with a black beard began speaking.

"We have to constantly see and evaluate life with the eyes of a child," he was saying. "Philosophers, such as Jesus Christ, have long known this to be true. That's why Christ said the kingdom of heaven belonged to the children. The kingdom of heaven isn't some mythic place in the clouds, but it's right here on Earth, today, for anyone with imagination enough to see it!"

His words seemed strange and obviously flawed to her—heaven a "mythic" place? But everything was suddenly heady and overpowering—both the ideas and the marijuana smoke. She felt something like a spell falling over her, and wondered whether to resist or let it happen.

## What would you do?

*If she resists, turn to page 119.*
*If she lets it sweep over her, turn to page 81.*

"Uh, you guys? Listen, I, uh, think I'll stay here," Ann said, smiling timidly.

"Why?" asked Cora.

Now what would she say, without sounding like a dumb little goody-goody?

"I'll stay with you," Janene interjected, then turned to Cora. "We can make some fudge for when you get back."

"Suit yourselves," Cora said with a shrug. "But this is going to be really fun."

The others left in an exuberant cluster, and Ann turned to Janene with a little laugh of relief.

"Thanks for staying," she said. "That kind of thing just makes me feel sort of, I don't know ... weird."

"Yeah, me too," Janene agreed. "That stuff's about as much fun going to the orthodontist's. I mean, Hillary's bunch isn't so bad, and since we all go to school together we should just try to get along. That's what I think at least."

"Me too!" Ann said. She was sitting cross-legged on the floor and beat her fists on her knees for emphasis. "You may have noticed I'm not the most, well, outgoing person in the world, but I do try to be nice to everybody and to think about other people's feelings and stuff."

"I know you do. I've noticed that about you," Janene said, pulling her thick, dark hair back into the comb that held it off her face. "I always wanted to be your friend, because you seemed so sweet and everything. I was really happy when you invited me tonight."

They were still absorbed in conversation when the others arrived back, flushed from the sharp night air and ready to eat.

"Where's that fudge you promised us?" Cora demanded, hands on her hips.

Ann and Janene exchanged a horrified look, then laughed.

"We had more important things to do," Janene said, and Ann nodded agreement. Beginning a new, strong friendship was the most important thing she could imagine.

■

Over the next weeks, Janene and Ann became closer and closer. Ann had never imagined how wonderful it could feel to have a friend she could trust with her deepest thoughts and

dreams like she trusted Janene. Or to have someone to share a joke with or a hot fudge sundae or even to cry with at sad movies. She and Janene thought they'd be best friends forever.

And then Janene's father was transferred.

"We're moving in three weeks," Janene told Ann over the phone, sounding choked up. "Oh, Ann, I'm going to miss you so much!"

Ann was nearly overwhelmed with sadness and loss. Janene was the one close friend she'd ever had, and she didn't know if she could make other friends. Should she even try? Or should she pull in and keep her loneliness tight inside?

---

## What would you do?

*If Ann reaches out to another group of kids, turn to page 90.*
*If she decides to go it alone, turn to page 33.*

"Well, yeah, sure. I mean, I guess I can, uh, come over," Ann stammered, still off-balance but with her sense of gloom quickly turning to excitement.

"Great!" Tara told her the address and hung up with a final friendly "Hurry, okay?"

Driving to Tara's, the usual self-doubts crowded into Ann's mind. Why had Tara asked *her*, of all people?

Finally, weary of her own putdowns, she got tough with the brown-eyed girl in the rearview mirror. "Why not you?" she asked herself out loud. "You're a nice person. There's no reason why people won't like you if you give them the chance and don't hide in your room like a little mouse all the time. Go for it!"

But her pep talk faded from memory when she reached Tara's house. It was practically a mansion! Tall, white columns lined the porch, with balconies extending from several different glass doorways upstairs. The immaculate, tree-lined lawn could've easily served as a putting green. The only pavement was a long, winding driveway that disappeared somewhere in back of the house. Ann checked the address twice, her heart pounding. How could she possibly even get up the nerve to walk into such a classy place?

But just then, Tara bounded out onto the wide front porch.

"Park it, Ann!" she called through cupped hands. "This is the place!"

■

Once inside, Tara escorted Ann down several hallways lined with expensive-looking artifacts and sculptures, and let Ann take in every room—from the private sauna in the guest bath to the cozy fireplace in the master bedroom.

"This place is incredible," Ann said after she'd received the tour, which ended on the pool deck behind the house. "Really, just great. I can't believe you've even got a pool."

"Yeah," Tara said, flopping down in a lawn chair with a bored sigh. "My parents live at their offices, so I'll have it to my-self this summer. Mom still commutes to work in Chicago. She's only home weekends. Some weekends. And Dad never gets home before 11 at night."

Ann nodded, trying not to show her surprise at the idea of Tara being home alone so much. "My folks are divorced, and Dad lives in Oregon," she told Tara. "Mom works as a clerk at the public library. She's home nights, though."

Tara shook her rich, auburn hair back from her shoulders. She looked like a model to Ann. Her clothes were so expensive. And her hair looked so shiny and soft. Maybe if you were that cool, that self-confident, you could afford to pick your friends without worrying about stuff like popularity.

"Hey, let's study out here, okay?" Tara jumped to her feet. "I'll get us some drinks."

"Great," Ann agreed. While Tara was gone to the kitchen, Ann leaned back in a lawn chair, closed her eyes and let the warm spring sunshine caress her face. She couldn't remember a more perfect morning. Unbelievable as it still seemed to her, Tara and she were actually becoming friends.

"Here you go." Ann opened her eyes, adjusted them to the glare and saw it was a wine cooler Tara held down toward her.

Ann gulped, completely thrown off by this new development. Ann was a Christian. She'd always believed drugs and drinking were stupid and destructive, and had never felt the slightest temptation to try anything like that. But this wasn't like "real" drinking, was it? It was more like a gesture of friendship. And wouldn't she look like a real jerk if she turned it down?

## What would you do?

*If Ann accepts the wine cooler, turn to page 9.*
*If she turns it down, turn to page 29.*

Ann decided the health of the relationship depended more on her than it did on Tara. After all, if Ann could stick by her beliefs, wouldn't that have to eventually influence Tara's actions, at least a little?

So Ann and Tara continued to spend time together, but Ann carefully avoided doing things with Tara that Ann felt compromised her faith. Tara came to respect Ann for her beliefs, and she and Ann would often spend long hours talking about Jesus' influence on Ann's life.

Years later, when Tara had married and moved to Georgia, she called Ann for one of their weekly long-distance chats and told her old friend some exciting news.

"Ann, I know you were always hoping I'd become a Christian," she began.

"I didn't exactly make a big secret of that," Ann laughed.

"No, you didn't," Tara agreed. "But you didn't push me too hard, either. I just watched you and saw how, well, solid it made you. And now, Todd and I have joined a church here."

"Oh, Tara, that's wonderful!"

"And I've accepted Christ," she said more softly. "You know, visiting your church with you off and on those years, I felt so close so many times. I was just afraid, I guess. Afraid of losing some imaginary freedom I thought I had. But now, I wonder why I waited. Now, I know what real freedom and happiness is all about."

"Yes," was all that Ann could manage through the lump in her throat. "Good, Tara. Yes."

The End

She shrugged and nodded slightly, too flustered to refuse. After all, she would only have to hold the beer, not drink it. Peter disappeared in the crowd and came right back, Ann's opened beer in one hand and a fresh one for himself in the other.

A few minutes later, there was a sharp knock at the front door—loud enough to be heard above the music. When someone casually threw it open, two police officers stood silhouetted against a glaring light outside. Instantly, somebody killed the stereo, and there was frightened silence in the room. The officers eyed the cooler of beer, then glanced around the room.

"Is there anyone over 18 on these premises?" the taller one asked sternly.

No one answered. "Uh, I can explain ... " Jamie began weakly.

But the other officer was already waving people out the door.

"You can do your explaining down at the station, son," he told Jamie. "And you others can call your parents from there too."

■

"I'm sorry, Mom," Ann whispered when they were in the car driving home.

Her mother cleared her throat, and spoke in a half-angry, half-hurt tone.

"Annie, I just don't understand. You were drinking? And there were no chaperones at the party at all? What were you ... what were you thinking?"

Ann stared out the car window, trying not to cry. Why did every attempt she made to fit in end up in disaster?

"I went with Rachelle. I didn't know what kind of party it was. I just wanted to belong ... somewhere. I hated it at that awful party, but ... " a tear streamed down her cheek. "Oh, I don't know. I guess I just don't fit in anywhere."

Mom pulled the car to the curb and turned off the motor. She took Ann in her arms. After a few moments, she said, "Annie, don't you know how special you are? It just takes time for people to see that. Just wait, honey. People will find you. You don't have to change for anyone. Okay?" She looked into Ann's eyes.

"Okay, Mom. Sure."

■

Ann was drying the dishes that night when Rachelle and her mother stopped by. While Mrs. Washington and Mom talked in the kitchen, Ann and Rachelle went on the front porch.

"Ann, I wanted to apologize for getting you into that mess today," Rachelle began. "I wanted to explain earlier, before we went to the party, but there wasn't time. It's just that, well, I don't really like the stuff my friends are into now—the drinking, the rowdiness. I know I need to make a break, but it's kind of scary, you know?"

Ann nodded, not quite sure of where this was leading.

Rachelle looked at Ann for a moment, then walked over and sat down on the porch steps. Ann followed and sat down beside her.

"I was thinking," continued Rachelle, looking down. "Well, if we—you and me, I mean—if we kind of hung out together, then neither of us would have to deal with all that stuff anymore. Does that make sense?"

"You mean, you want to be friends?"

Ann knew she sounded a little goofy, but it seemed too good to be true.

"Maybe we could plan our own party, even invite Jamie and the others," Rachelle continued excitedly. "But no booze. You know, maybe a picnic or something. What do you think, Ann? Does that sound stupid?"

"Uh, no." A little voice in Ann's head began ranting at her, telling her that Rachelle was just using her to appease her mom or that Rachelle wouldn't really like her after she got to know her. But, using Rachelle's "trick," she shushed that voice.

"Your plan sounds great. Count me in," she said happily.

There were several other alcohol-free parties after that first one—each one bigger than the last. Eventually, through the influence of the parties, some of Jamie's friends even started coming to youth group. As for Rachelle and Ann, they started doing more things together and, over time, became the best of friends.

The End

No, it was absolutely ridiculous to think that she could've helped Tara. Tara was obviously out of it to begin with—period. Either that, or her drowning was accidental—pure and simple. Ann had had nothing—nothing!—to do with it.

From then on she never talked about Tara's death or let anyone else mention it around her. But she started having nightmares about it many nights, horrible dreams where she was trapped by tons of water and could see light above her but couldn't reach it. And her stomach began to hurt.

Her stomachaches began to worsen a week or so after the coroner found conclusively that Tara's death had been suicide. Her head hurt a lot now too and, feeling stressed out and miserable, Ann hid a bottle of cheap wine in her closet and drank a little. A drink would usually make her head feel better, temporarily, but it made her stomach hurt even worse.

A week before Thanksgiving vacation her senior year, Ann collapsed at school with a bleeding ulcer and was rushed to the hospital. Recovering, she spent some long, quiet afternoons in the little chapel there. And it was on one of those afternoons, as she sat quietly looking at the cross above the small altar, that she felt the truth she'd tried to deny rising to the surface.

"Tara, I'm sorry I wasn't the friend you needed to have," she whispered, and everything inside her broke. She buried her face in her hands and sobbed until her strength was gone.

She knew she was forgiven then, but still she would never think of Tara without regret. In the years to come, she often thought about that hospital chapel and how God met her there—despite her awful mistakes—and held her. And healed her broken heart.

And maybe, just maybe, she thought, God could use her now ... to meet other people, and hold them, and help God heal their brokenness too. At least she wanted to try—out of love for God.

And for Tara.

The End

"That was *so* fun!" Tara beamed on the drive home. "Thanks for inviting me tonight, Ann. I'd really like to start coming to youth group all the time."

"I'll just bet you would." Ann forced the words through a hot lump in her throat.

For a couple of blocks there was a strained silence while Ann clutched the steering wheel so hard she thought it might break in half.

Finally, Tara cleared her throat and asked softly, "Ann, are you mad at me?"

Was it possible Tara didn't know what she'd done? Could she be that blind, that insensitive? But a small voice in Ann's head told her that was unfair. After all, it wasn't Tara's fault she was pretty and outgoing. And, really, how could she have possibly known Jason was the guy Ann's heart was set on?

"Tara, I just don't know if this will work," Ann began, her voice shaking a little. "You and me being friends, I mean. We just have nothing in common. You're so pretty, and I'm just plain and dull. You're like, well, like caviar or something rich and rare. And I'm like a can of sardines by comparison."

For a second, Tara looked confused. Then she burst into laughter, clutching her stomach when she could hardly get her breath.

"Oh, great. Fine. Just laugh," Ann said, furious now. Tears burned behind her eyes. "You and Jason can maybe go out somewhere this week and just laugh your heads off at me, together."

Tara's laughter stopped immediately. "Oh, no, Ann. Is Jason your ... boyfriend?" she asked quietly.

Ann didn't answer. One fat tear leaked dramatically down her right cheek, and she let her chin quiver a little.

"Oh, Ann, I'm so sorry I flirted with him like I did," Tara said quickly, sounding really ashamed. "I honestly had no idea. It's just that ... well, you're so smart, and everybody obviously likes to be with you. And I guess I was showing off because I felt so inferior. If you don't want me for a friend, I'll understand. I guess I should've known that somebody as together as you doesn't need a flake like me hanging around."

Tara's words shocked Ann out of her self-pity. Her tears stopped. She even forgot to make her chin quiver.

"Me—together? That's a joke. Just look at me." She began wiping her tears with the back of her hand.

Tara turned in her seat to lean toward her. "Ann, I don't think you realize how people see you. You seem so steady. I wish I had your resolve and the courage to stick up for what you believe in." Tara grinned slightly. "But most of the time I feel like a boneless chicken."

Ann and Tara looked at each other for a second or two, then burst out laughing. The girls decided to stop in a fast-food drive-in for a Coke. Then they parked in the lot and just talked.

Something almost imperceivable happened that night. You could hear it in the silence between words and feel it in the warmth of the girls' hearts. They both knew something had changed. Sure, there would be other arguments and more hurt feelings as time went on. But the bond of friendship they sealed that night would weather them all. For Tara and Ann had learned the secret of true communication—speaking with honesty from the heart. And whatever happened from now on, they were—first and foremost—true friends.

The End

Still, the idea of spending the night with Tim was totally out of the question! It went against every conviction she had.

"You mean, the boys are staying all night?" Ann asked.

"That's the whole idea," Tara said brightly, then caught a look at the stunned expression on Ann's face. "Hey, don't tell me you have some kind of hang-up about that."

"Tara, I can't spend the night out here with Tim!" Ann said. "I didn't dream that ..."

"Listen." Tara had her hands on her hips and spoke inches from Ann's face. "Number one, lower your voice, would you please? And number two, I've waited all week for this chance to be with Roger, and I won't have anything—or anybody—messing it up."

Ann shook her head. "I can't stay, Tara. I just can't."

"Fine!" Tara kicked the wastebasket, hard, on her way out the restroom door. "Then call your mommy and have her come pick you up, because we're leaving for the lake house—with or without you."

■

"I'm sorry, Mom." Ann's voice was husky with misery as she sat in the car with Mom at the wheel. "I know you had better ways to use your Saturday night than to drive 50 miles to bring me home."

"No problem," Mom said gently. "I just wish you'd mentioned that there would be boys when you asked my permission."

"You wouldn't have given it, would you?" Ann asked quietly.

"No, I wouldn't have," Mom responded. "Annie, I guess I sort of judge your friends by the effect they have on you. And if a friend is going to make you feel you have to sneak around and even lie to me, well then ..."

"I know," Ann whispered. "I've already decided Tara and I are too different. I guess I can't trust her."

They drove in silence for a few minutes, then Mom cleared her throat.

"You know, Annie, there are so many girls you could make friends with, but you never invite anyone over. Why not have a slumber party or something like that?"

She shrugged, looking out the window. "No one would come."

"Oh, Annie, sure they would. You've already had a couple of girls from church calling you, haven't you?"

"Yeah." Ann turned to her. "You really think they'd come?"

Mom smiled and nodded encouragingly.

Again they rode in silence for a while, then Ann cleared her throat. "So you really think I should throw a party, huh?"

Mom smiled. "I'll help, okay?"

■

To Ann's happy surprise, when she began calling that week, six people quickly told her they'd love to come to her party. Only two turned her down, and only because they were going to Hillary Stanton's birthday party that same night.

Ann was nervous all week, especially Friday afternoon as she checked and rechecked her food supplies and made triple sure she'd remembered to rent videos. She tried not to panic when her mind touched the possibility that everybody would be bored at her party.

But that didn't happen. From the minute the six other girls arrived, there was so much silliness and goofing around that Ann couldn't even find time to start any of the three movies. She quickly realized it was just being together that was fun, not the "props" she'd thought she'd have to rely on.

At a certain point in the evening, the talk began to center on the other party in town that night—Hillary Stanton's.

"I guess most of the popular kids are there." Cora Bagis threw a piece of caramel corn into the air and caught it in her mouth. "I bet they're all comparing fakey smiles."

"Ooooo!" Ginger Edwards giggled. "You look truly divine. And don't you look sweet!" Ginger tried a husky imitation of Bette Midler, but nobody caught it.

"Well it's true that Hillary and her friends are a bunch of snobs," Cora said with a shrug. "You ever notice how Hillary always has her mirror out? I think the woman has gone over the edge."

Stacy Powell, giggling, threw a pillow toward Cora, lost her balance and somersaulted off the bed. "You know what we ought to do? We ought to go over there and crash their party!"

"Yeah!" Janene Grant shouted from where she was sitting cross-legged on Ann's vanity table. "We could sneak around under the windows and find out what they look like without the tons of makeup they wear! We could even make scary noises so they'd think Hillary's fancy split-level house is haunted!"

She did a gruesome Boris Karloff imitation, and everybody rolled around howling with laughter at their own silly plans.

Ann couldn't be sure if they were serious about any of this, but it was making her uneasy. For one thing, she didn't like gossiping, and Hillary and her gang seemed okay to her. Not the most friendly kids in school, maybe a bit stuck-up. But basically okay.

"Listen you guys, I rented these neat movies ... " she began, hoping to put the party on a different track.

"Time for movies later, Ann," Cora said, jumping to her feet. "Okay, who's coming to Hillary's?"

"But what'll we do there?" Janene asked. "Seriously. What?"

Cora, grinning slyly, slipped dramatically into the bathroom adjoining Ann's room and was back in a flash.

"Voilà!" She produced two rolls of toilet paper from behind her back. "We'll stop by 7-11 for more of this stuff and T.P. her yard! Think of the fun everybody will have tomorrow morning! Can't you just picture Hillary and her friends jerking soggy paper out of her trees and trying not to mess up their perfect hair at the same time?"

Again, all the girls bent double with giggles, then started hunting for their shoes and jackets.

It seemed like a crummy idea to Ann, but she hated to be a party pooper—especially at her own party.

## What would you do?

*If Ann goes along to T.P. Hillary's house, turn to page 70.*
*If she stays behind while the others go, turn to page 47.*

Rachelle folded her arms and frowned thoughtfully. "Sometimes I look at us all sitting in our pew during the worship service, and I wonder what we look like to a teenage visitor in our church. We may be like the 'in crowd' table in the school cafeteria, where they almost have a sign over their heads that reads 'By invitation only.' Maybe Ann's right and we should try to reach out a little more."

"Okay, but how?" Randy asked. "Don't you need a plan for reaching out?"

"Nothing boring," Cora said quickly. "We need a plan with pizazz."

"Pizazz?" Randy asked, making a goofy face. Rachelle giggled and gently slapped him on the arm.

"Well, how about a party?" Ann suggested, nervously clearing her throat. "We could, uh, invite all the kids in town—make it really open."

"Hey, that sounds like fun," Cora chimed in. "Let's do that. But you know, no beer and stuff. Just music and food."

"Yeah, right." countered Randy. "But the real question is whether Reverend Sumner will go for it."

"One way to find out," Mrs. Rossmond said with a twinkle in her eye. "He's probably in his study right now."

◼

"You know, this is a great idea!" Reverend Sumner put his feet on his desk, crossed his ankles, and leaned back with a dreamy smile on his face. "I'd like to see you kids organize a community-wide event like you're talking about. The fellowship hall would be the perfect place for a big bash like that."

Jason looked at Ann and raised his eyebrows.

"You and the church council would really let us run it and plan it and everything?" Jason asked. "You'd let us decorate like we wanted and get potato chips on the floor and play the music loud as we could stand it ... er, I mean, loud as anybody wanted it?"

Reverend Sumner chuckled. "Yes to all three things. And we'd even chip in to help you rent a nice big sound system. The church will provide plates, cups, napkins, ice—things like that."

"I'll head the publicity!" Cora bounced in her chair. "Who wants to help with posters?"

Several hands shot up.

"Music? Who has the best tape collection?"

"Maybe we should see if we can get a Christian rock group to come for a couple of hours!"

"Maybe we should have pizza!"

"No, Mexican food!"

"Both! And hot dogs!"

Reverend Sumner slipped quietly from behind his desk and left his study to the kids.

■

Ann was thrilled to be a part of the action, and eagerly helped take care of decorations and publicity over the next three weeks. By party night, the fellowship hall had transformed, with a sound system monopolizing one wall and food tables lining another. Three pingpong tables were huddled in one section of the room, and Randy even had the great idea of renting a big-screen television to set up in the lobby.

"What if nobody shows up after all this work?" Cora asked that evening, nervously gnawing a thumbnail.

## Blind choice:

*Without looking ahead, turn to page 101 or page 117 to continue the story.*

"Tara, I don't know how to act around them!"

Ann, in Tara's car outside Hillary's house that Sunday night, was having a minor panic attack.

"Just be yourself, Ann! And if that doesn't work, have a glass or two of wine to loosen up. It won't hurt you."

Tara got out from in front of the steering wheel of her red convertible, and Ann scrambled out her door and followed meekly up the walk. The house was practically throbbing with rock music from Hillary's super-size sound system. Hillary had invited most of Crestview High's football team—the male equivalents of her own group—so couples leaned together and tried to dance a little in the crowd. It was too loud for real conversation, a relief to Ann. Still, remembering Tara's advice, she took a glass of wine from a well-stocked bar in the corner of the huge rec room. She figured that although she didn't drink, this was one time when she needed help to relax.

Later she didn't remember a thing of what she'd said or done—the wine tasted just like strong grape juice, and before she knew it she'd downed three glasses. But she must've passed the audition, because Monday, Tara and a couple of the others waved and signaled for her to sit at their table in the cafeteria.

She was "in"! She was actually a popular girl!

The prospect was so exciting and unbelievable that she didn't stop to question whether she wanted to be.

It didn't take her long to learn that to fit in with her new friends, she had to constantly be "on," constantly witty and ready with comments and jokes. Any uncool move brought the ridicule of the others, like the time she'd declined to let Hillary copy from her on a history test and all the gang had given her the silent treatment until she apologized. Sometimes the pressure made her want to hide in a stall in the restroom.

Still, it dazzled her to think about her new status. She'd achieved everybody's dream. She, Ann Tyler, belonged!

■

"How come you don't come to youth group anymore, Ann?" Rachelle asked her in the hall one day. It wasn't the first time one of her old friends had accosted her. Ann, a little irritated, wondered how they could possibly consider youth group carwashes and pizza parties to be more important than being popular.

"Well, you know, I'm really busy these days," Ann said, copying Hillary's breezy manner.

At first, Ann felt guilty neglecting church stuff, but she'd thought it through and figured since God wanted the best for her, he'd want her to be with the right crowd—obviously. Church didn't happen to be compatible with that. But later in her life she'd start attending again. She was sure God understood all that. Still, her Christian friends just wouldn't seem to give up.

Well, that was their problem, not hers.

Generally, Ann tried not to give herself much time to think about her new friends and church. If she did, the heebie-jeebies crept in and made her wonder if she was really living now or just acting. If she was having fun, or just pretending to so she'd stay securely "in." It was all pretty confusing.

Wine held down the heebie-jeebies. So did No Doz pills. One mellowed her, the other made her a little high. Either would temporarily help make her who she needed to be to fit in, so she kept a secret stash of both.

■

And then, without warning, Ann's father died in an accident at the paper mill where he worked. He'd been living in Oregon since his divorce from Ann's mother, so Ann hadn't seen him often the past couple of years. Still, she loved him. And she was stunned with pain and loss.

Mom had had her own complicated feelings about Ann's father and retreated into shocked silence for a time. Besides, she and Ann had grown farther and farther apart since Ann's split with the church. Ann couldn't take her mother's constant nagging and so had shut her out months ago.

But now, Ann felt terrifyingly alone with her grief. She needed someone to help her through this. Of course her friends were the logical place to turn, but she wasn't sure. Would they support her or only make things worse by thinking it was no big deal? Could she risk having them react that way?

## What would you do?

*If Ann turns to her friends, turn to page 125.*
*If she can't risk their indifference, turn to page 97.*

"That was really fun," Tara said in Ann's car on the drive home. "I'd like to start coming to youth group—will you pick me up next week?"

"I doubt if I can," Ann said sharply, too angry to say anything more. She frowned grimly at the road in front of her. She knew she was being rude. But not as rude as Tara had been, openly flirting with Jason.

"Oh," Tara said, confused. "Oh, well, uh, okay."

Tara called a few times over the next weeks, but Ann brushed her off each time. She quit picking up Tara on Sunday mornings too. Tara came to church a couple of times alone, then quit. When Ann began to feel guilty about that, she just remembered the pain she'd felt, watching Tara and Jason alone in the youth room corner.

By the time school let out for summer break, Tara had quit calling. Ann had a job as an assistant coach for the children's tennis team and was too busy to think of Tara, or much of anything else. Then one July night, riffling through the Crestview Herald News, Ann read Tara's obituary.

Drowned. Family pool. Drowned.

■

Ann felt a haze settle over her that night that deepened the next few days. Around town, she heard people calling Tara's death suicide. A vision of Tara by the pool, alone and with a wine cooler in her hand, seared into Ann's brain, though she tried to shut that picture—and a few others involving Tara—firmly out.

Finally, after several sleepless nights, Ann asked herself the question she'd been avoiding. Could she have been responsible—even a little responsible—for Tara's death?

## What would you do?

*If Ann blames herself for Tara's suicide, turn to page 36.*
*If she decides she couldn't have helped, turn to page 55.*

"Listen, you guys, maybe it would help if we had some meetings and studied this a little more," Ann suggested with surprising boldness.

A few people began to talk about Ann's suggestion—at least nobody said anything to refute it right away. But several people eventually said they didn't think meetings like that would make a difference.

"It's just too hard to reach some people," Randy Miller summed up. "I think your friend may be a lost cause."

While they'd been talking, Chris had slipped quietly into the small kitchen that joined the youth room and started rummaging in the cabinet over the sink. Just as Randy spoke, Chris returned to the circle with a metal spice can, shook something from it into his hand and blew. The tiny seeds scattered and came to rest on jeans, in hair and on the already-messy squares of carpet.

"Hey!" Randy protested. "These are new jeans! What is this stuff?"

"Mustard seeds," Chris said. "If you have faith as a grain of mustard seed, you can move mountains—remember?"

"And they're so tiny ... " Ann breathed. Then everybody was quiet for a while, until Jason broke the silence.

"Maybe a study wouldn't be such a bad idea. I think we need to take a look at our attitudes and try to discover what God thinks about all this."

■

"Friendship evangelism," Chris said the next week. "That's our subject tonight. You may not consider the friendships you have to be tools for reaching out with God's message, but they really are. Very effective tools. Tools that can change the world."

"For good *or* bad," Randy interjected. "I mean, our witness can go against us, if we profess to be Christians but don't act like Christians, right?"

"Good point." Chris nodded. "Really, all of us may as well have the word 'Christian' painted across our T-shirt. You're witnessing all the time—for better or worse. And when you're around your friends—people who respect your opinion and your thoughts—your witness is especially powerful. Ann, that friend of yours you talked about last week may secretly be yearning for someone to prove her wrong. You said she thinks non-Christians are fakes. Well, maybe that's a perfect opening for you to step in and show her through your own sincerity that we're not."

Ann remembered the wine cooler, something she'd been trying hard to block out. Tara had witnessed a false side of Ann last week. Chris was right—now it was time to try to undo that damage and show Tara who the real Ann Tyler was.

There were a couple of youth group activities coming up, and Ann decided she would definitely get up her nerve and invite Tara to one of them. The only question was which—a pizza party at the church or a movie party at Crestview Cinema?

## What would you do?

*If Ann invites Tara to a pizza party, turn to page 74.*
*If she invites her to a movie, turn to page 79 .*

By the time she found Tara rummaging in her locker after school, Ann was shaking with anger.

"How could you?" she sobbed. "How could you lie like that?"

"Oh, quit whining for a change." Tara didn't even turn toward her, just kept plowing through her pile of books.

"Look at me!" Ann spit out, grabbing her arm. "Answer me!"

Tara slapped her hand away angrily. "Leave me alone, little crybaby!" She shoved at Ann. "Why should I have to answer to you for anything I do?"

Ann, hurt and furious, shocked herself by shoving back. In seconds, the two girls were engaged in a pushing and slapping match that was only broken up when the principal, Mrs. Shandish, came hurrying out of her office and grabbed each by an arm.

■

"Annie, you've got to get a hold of yourself," Mom said, frustrated, in the car. The girls had each been given a three-day suspension, and calling Mom to take her home had been agony for Ann.

"I ... I know," she murmured, hiccuping with sobs. "But I ... hate her, Mom! I do! I hate her!"

"Now, Annie, hate never accomplishes anything. Don't you remember Jesus' teaching about ... "

"Mom, if you tell me to turn the other cheek, I'll scream!"

Mom, taking a deep breath, was silent, and Ann stared miserably out the windshield. A couple of minutes passed before Mom dared try to make her point again.

"Honey, I was just going to remind you that your anger and hatred will hurt you far more than they can hurt Tara. Jesus knew that and wanted us to live without such negative, draining emotions controlling us. He came to give us love, because love is always stronger than hate."

"But she turned everybody against me, Mom! Everybody believes that I stole those things!"

Mom turned the corner of their street. Ann squinted—three kids were gathered in front of their house.

"It's kids from the youth group ... " Ann breathed, straining forward in her seat. "What are they doing here?"

Mom pulled into the driveway, and Ann got slowly from the car. The kids approached her, smiling, obviously sympathetic.

"We ... we want you to know we don't believe those stupid rumors, and we're going to help set them straight, Ann," Rachelle said as the others nodded.

Ann felt her face stretch into a relieved grin, and she glanced at Mom, who grinned back and winked.

Ann saw that day that Mom had been right. Love *was* stronger than hate. It has a way of covering over mistakes and seeing through lies.

Ann saw Tara again after that day, even waved hello to her in the halls. At first, Tara couldn't figure out what Ann was up to. But eventually, she gave up trying to figure it out. For some reason, Ann had decided to forgive Tara and had even begun to reach out to her again.

It wasn't too long before the two girls were out scanning the mall again, talking and joking and having fun.

And somewhere in Tara's heart, she wondered what kind of love constantly motivated Ann not to give up on her and to always care like she did.

The End

Ann battled with her pesky conscience during the drive to the 7-11 and then to Hillary's house—and finally won. In fact, she thought it was kind of fun throwing the toilet paper rolls through the dark trees and watching them cascade down. It was even more fun running with the others, crouched like giggling bandits, back to their car. Somehow their little adventure seemed to bind them closer, and the rest of the night they talked about everything—as if they'd been a tight group for ages.

Over the next weeks, Ann was invited to the other six girls' houses. Often they'd entertain themselves by sneaking around, like the T.P. episode at her slumber party. For instance, one night they snuck out with Janene's father's new car and went cruising. Another time they anonymously called some of Hillary's crowd and told them they'd seen their boyfriends with other girls. That kind of thing was fun—the danger of getting caught, the freedom of breaking the rules.

And then one night, Traci Chandler called. The seven girls more or less paired up, switching often, and she was Ann's best buddy at the moment.

"Ann, I'm spending the night with Todd, but I told Mom I was going to be with you. So if she calls, say I'm in the bathroom or something. Okay?"

## What would you do?

*If Ann agrees to cover for Traci, turn to page 76.*
*If she refuses, turn to page 111.*

But just when Ann had almost summoned the courage to make her suggestion, Randy Miller spoke.

"We're so close and supportive the way we are that I'd hate for an outsider to come in being all sarcastic and everything and mess that up, know what I mean?"

Nods of agreement brought the subject to a quick close.

A few weeks later, Ann, Randy, Jason, Cora and a few others were visiting in their classroom before Sunday school, when Mrs. Rossmond entered the room and said a strange thing.

"Well, I see the gang's all here. But I've been wondering— has anybody invited anyone new to join us lately?"

They looked at each other and frowned.

Cora smiled. "What do you mean? Everybody knows they can come here. You can read it in foot-high letters on the sign right outside the church—Welcome!"

Ann thought of Tara and felt a little twinge of lingering guilt. Was their church group really becoming an exclusive clique?

"Still, I guess we could actually invite some of the other kids, couldn't we?" she asked meekly.

---

### Blind choice:

*Without looking ahead, turn to page 61 or page 43 to continue the story.*

"Thanks for inviting me, Hillary. But I've got youth group at church that night."

Hillary looked stunned. Her mouth flew so wide open her gum nearly dropped out.

"Okay, fine," she said a little sarcastically and sashayed on down the hall. Ann, watching her go, realized Hillary may never have had anyone turn her down before. Well, there was a first time for everything. And that thought made Ann smile.

■

At youth group Sunday, Rachelle Washington invited Ann to come over the next afternoon to study for a history test. That's what they were doing when some of Rachelle's friends called and told her they were getting together at a friend's house.

"It's at Jamie White's house. They really want us to come!" Rachelle whispered to Ann, covering the phone.

"Us?" Ann asked, knowing the invitation had only been for Rachelle.

Rachelle uncovered the receiver and told Jamie they'd be there in a few minutes. She raised her eyebrows toward Ann for confirmation, and Ann nodded timidly.

"Wow," Ann said uneasily when Rachelle hung up the phone. "I hope I know what to say to those kids."

"Listen," Rachelle said softly, "I feel self-conscious around new people too. There's a little voice inside my head that tells me I should be scared, but I just tell it to shush. Then I mentally repeat my good, strong qualities to myself. Try that, it might work for you too."

"Okay," Ann said without much commitment.

Rachelle grabbed her purse. "At least Jamie only lives a few blocks from you, so you can go home whenever you want."

■

When Rachelle parked at Jamie's curb, pounding music from inside the house reached out and surrounded the car.

"Get in here!" Jamie and a couple of other guys yelled from the front porch. They all three had beers in their hands, and Jamie was smoking.

"All right!" Joe Armando called over Jamie's shoulder. "Chicas mas finas!"

A couple of girls, overhearing, came out of the house and jumped Joe from behind, tickling him and yelling that he was a male-chauvinist pig and they were going to teach him a lesson.

"All right!" he yelled happily as they drug him back into the house. "I like it! I like it!"

"Well," Rachelle said, taking a deep breath and opening her car door. "Ready for this?"

It was dark in the house—all the curtains were drawn, and there was lots of smoke. You could tell right away there were no adults anywhere around—too many couples openly necking for that. In one corner sat a big cooler full of beer. In another, the stereo system throbbed out walls of sound.

James Harper came over, put his arm around Rachelle's shoulders and led her away. She looked back at Ann and shot her a "sorry but I'll see you later" smile. A few seconds later, Peter Thompson came up and leaned against the part of the wall where Ann was trying to dissolve into the woodwork. He bent close to her, winked and held up his beer.

"Want one?" he mouthed.

A beer was the thing Ann wanted least in the world, but she didn't know what to do. Even though she never drank, maybe she should just hold one, so she wouldn't feel so conspicuous. Or maybe she should just get out of here and not worry about explanations.

## What would you do?

*If Ann decides to make an escape, turn to page 112.*
*If she stays awhile, turn to page 53.*

"A pizza party? I love pizza!" Tara said over the phone.

"Great. I'll pick you up Wednesday afternoon at about 5:30, okay? And Tara—wear grubbies. Things can get a little crazy when the whole youth group is crammed into the church kitchen. A few of the kids think cooking is a sports activity."

"Gotcha," Tara laughed.

Ann was smiling as she hung up the phone. Tara hadn't stalled at the idea of coming to the church again. It would be so great if the kids in the group could blast away her stereotyped ideas about "church things" right on their home turf.

■

"Mamma mia!" Randy Miller chortled. "Watcha this, bambinos!"

He threw the pizza dough he was tossing so high a glob of it stuck to the kitchen ceiling, and the rest came down in a damp glump on the floor.

"Uh oh," he mumbled as the others cracked up.

"Are you sure you're a genuine Italian, Randy?" Tom asked suspiciously, plopping anchovies in spirals on the pie he and Tara were working on.

"I swear it." Randy solemnly crossed his heart. "I lived in Rome, Georgia, for nearly three years when I was little."

Again, everyone laughed. Jason Kyle swung open the oven door, and the smell made everyone groan with hunger. He pulled out the two pizza sculptures he and Ann had lovingly crafted— one shaped like a heart, the other shaped like ... something.

"See my Porsche?" He proudly held up the second pizza for everyone's approval. "I can't decide whether to eat it or take it to the track."

"I can sort of make out sausage wheels ..." Cora Bagis conceded kindly. But the others shook their heads decisively and gave it the thumbs-down sign.

"Don't worry, Jason. It'll definitely taste better than it looks," Tara sympathized. "It would have to."

The others laughed, and Jason held his pizza Porsche to Tara, offering her the first bite. She took a huge mouthful, and giggled as cheese strung down her chin. It was the first time Ann had seen her forget about her perfect looks and just let herself have fun. It struck her that that's what real friendship could do for you—it could let you forget about all the poses and masks and just be yourself.

◼

"That was really neat," Tara told Ann as they pulled into her driveway a few hours later. "And that pizza was delicious, even though I'm so stuffed I'll probably look like a blimp in my swim-suit this weekend. Which reminds me—my parents said I could invite you to come with me to our lake house. We could go Saturday morning and come back Sunday night. How about it? It'd be fun—just one long party all weekend."

The invitation was tempting. But Ann had church obligations Sunday, including the outreach series at youth group.

## What would you do?

*If Ann goes with Tara to her lake house, turn to page 98.*
*If Ann invites Tara to her house and church instead, turn to page 123.*

After a second of hesitation, Ann agreed to do it. After all, what were real friends for if you couldn't trust them to keep your secrets? Besides, the chances were about a thousand to one that Mrs. Chandler would call to check up on Traci.

But she did call, at about 11:00 that night.

"Ann? Listen, put Traci on the phone. Quickly."

"She's ... in the bathroom," Ann said weakly. Mrs. Chandler's voice was shrill and shaky. Ann felt scared.

"Ann, this is an emergency. Traci's father's been in an automobile accident tonight and is at Mercy Hospital." Her voice faltered. Ann heard her gulp several quick gasps of air, then she went on, sobbing. "Ann, this is very serious. Get Traci on the phone for me, right now. Please!"

"She's not here," Ann pushed out. "She's at ... Todd's."

There was silence on the line, then Ann heard Mrs. Chandler crying more openly. She didn't say anything else, and Ann couldn't think of anything to say either. Then the phone clicked. Ann stared numbly at it for a few seconds, then hung it up. She had to go to Mercy Hospital. She had to be there for Traci.

But she had just been the one to tell Mrs. Chandler Traci was sleeping with her boyfriend, Todd. Would Traci blame her for that and think she'd been disloyal?

## Blind choice:

*Without looking ahead, turn to page 92 or page 114 to continue the story.*

"My parents like for us to go to our lake house a lot of Sunday afternoons, so anything Sunday night might be hard to swing," Tara said slowly. "But maybe I could start coming Sunday mornings some."

Ann was grinning ear to ear. "Yeah, that'd be great!"

■

Tara began coming with the Tylers every Sunday morning. Ann was so happy to have her in the church, and Tara seemed to be eagerly soaking everything in. In fact, she started putting out hints that she might be ready to give up her Sunday evenings at the lake in order to attend youth group.

"Mostly my parents and their friends just sit around and drink and talk, anyway," she finally told Ann wistfully. "I'm just in the way, and the booze really bothers me. Now, I mean."

Ann felt a lump come into her throat. Tara was growing spiritually by leaps and bounds. It was just a shame her parents weren't in this with her.

"Well, listen," Ann said, not wanting to push too hard, "the decision's up to you. But any time you want to try youth group, just give me a whistle and I'll pick you up for it."

Tara puckered her lips and gave out a weak, breathy sound. "Consider that a whistle, okay?" she laughed. "Can I tag along with you this week?"

■

Tara fit in well with the kids at youth group. Too well, in fact.

Jason Kyle, a boy Ann had a secret crush on for ages, couldn't take his eyes off Tara. And she flirted back every chance she got.

"We need to make plans for the carwash next month," Chris Peters, their youth minister, told them. "Let's break into small groups and do a little brainstorming, okay?"

Jason went over and grabbed Tara's hand, pulling her into a corner of the room. "We're one team!" he called over his shoulder, and Tara nodded eagerly along.

They sat huddled there the rest of the evening, laughing and talking intensely about things Ann was positive had nothing whatsoever to do with washing cars.

By the time youth group was finally over, Ann was seething. How insensitive could Tara be? It really hurt seeing Jason monopolized like this, and if Tara was a real friend she'd be able to see that!

## What would you do?

*If Ann talks to Tara about her feelings, turn to page 56.*
*If she keeps them inside and snubs her, turn to page 65.*

"A movie party?" Tara questioned over the phone.

"Yeah, there's that new adventure movie on at the Crestview Cinema, then we're planning to eat afterward. We'd really like you to come, Tara."

"Well, I don't know ... "

"Come on. It'll be fun."

"Well, okay." Tara finally answered with a laugh. "I just hope I can behave myself around you Christians. I'd hate to corrupt anybody."

Ann thought she heard a hint of real fear behind Tara's wise-crack, and she was glad she'd chosen the movie party, where Tara could get to know the others without the church building itself making her paranoid. For the first time, Ann thought about how it must feel to be a non-Christian, raised in a home where God's Word was conspicuously absent. It's easy to see how someone like that might feel judged or inferior around Christians, just be-cause of her background.

But Ann was proud of the way the kids welcomed and in-luded Tara the night of the movie party. Cora Bagis and Rachelle Washington saved Ann and Tara two seats, and the four of them shared a super-jumbo popcorn, giggling as they passed the huge, greasy container back and forth. At Taco Casa after the movie, Randy Miller proposed a taco-eating contest and asked Tara to be official scorekeeper. She laughingly agreed.

"I just couldn't believe it when Randy ate that seventh taco!" Tara laughed, as she and Ann drove home afterward. "And the way you guys cheered him on—boy, what a bunch of maniacs! I was expecting the guy to blow up at any moment!"

Ann smiled. "Nah, we've seen him eat nine without even loosening his belt. So you had a good time?"

"Yeah, I did." Tara said, still smiling. "I was surprised I did, but I really did."

"Why surprised?" Ann tried to sound casual.

Tara looked thoughtful as she spoke. "I guess I expected a little of the old 'holier-than-thou' treatment. But your friends are really nice."

"Yeah, they are," Ann responded, feeling proud that Tara called them *her* friends. "We're just glad to have you with us."

Tara chewed her lip momentarily, then said, "I also think it's pretty amazing that you all manage to, well, have such a good time together without ... getting into lots of stuff. No drinking, I mean. Stuff like that. Heck, I didn't even hear a cuss word all night! It kind of felt ... good. You know what I mean?"

"Oh, Tara, we'd love to have you start coming to church and youth group all the time!" Ann said quickly.

Ann thought she saw Tara flinch slightly. Was it surprise at her invitation or because she felt cornered? Ann worried that she'd pushed too hard and that Tara would feel rushed now. Or would she recognize Ann's sincerity and the genuine friendship the others had offered tonight, and appreciate the invitation?

## Blind choice:

*Without looking ahead, turn to page 77 or page 87 to continue the story.*

She sat back and got such a deep lung full of the pungent smoke that she coughed, then giggled. A few seconds ago she'd thought that if she stayed she might challenge some of the ideas floating around, but now that seemed unimportant. And besides, she couldn't get the words straight. Everything was tumbling in her brain.

She just felt like giggling and giggling. When the boy next to her saw that, he giggled too and offered a sip of his wine.

She drank, and when the wine got to her, she tried a tiny smoke of marijuana. It burned and made her cough some more, but for the first time ever she didn't feel self-conscious in a crowd. And that seemed absolutely wonderful.

The next day at school, the boy who'd been sitting next to her and shared his wine—Nicky Manscotti—came up to her locker and, putting his arm briefly around her waist, told her he hoped she'd come to another meeting. Ann felt exhilarated all week.

The only dark cloud was that at youth group Sunday night, she felt sort of funny, dishonest or something. Like she was living two lives. She wondered if anyone there had tried marijuana.

And when she told them a little about the discussion they'd had at the meeting, which she had decided had been worthwhile and stimulating, they put it down.

"Hey everybody, I realized something this week about that passage in Matthew where Jesus is talking about little children," she'd said. "You know, Jesus says the children will inherit the kingdom of heaven, so that means heaven is really here on Earth. Because little kids are so full of wonder and everything, and so much a part of the Earth. Get it?"

Everyone looked confused. A few shook their heads.

"Ann, where'd you get this stuff?" Randy Miller asked.

"It's not *stuff* Randy! It's philosophy!"

Driving home, she couldn't seem to put her thoughts together. She felt like her new friendships and her old friendships in youth group were on a collision course. But then again, maybe she could be true to her church beliefs and join the club too. Just no more marijuana or wine.

The next week at Philosophy Club she stuck to that policy, until Nicky leaned toward her, a fresh joint in his hand.

"Here you go, babe," he whispered, extending the marijuana toward her. His dark eyes were bright and the bones in his face so strong and handsome when he smiled at her just that way.

"Enjoy, Ann," Desiree said, sitting beside her at that same moment and giving her one of two glasses of wine she held.

Ann swallowed hard, then took the wine glass and clinked it against the one Desiree extended. Really, what harm would it do? And it would do a world of good in the friendship department. Ann could laugh and have fun so much easier with a little marijuana or wine or something.

■

"Annie, open this door. Tonight, we're talking." Mom leaned one ear against the wood of the door.

"I'm busy, Mom. Do me a favor and just go away, okay?"

"Now, young lady!"

With a deep sigh, Ann got off the bed, turned the stereo down a little and slouched over to open the lock. In the two months since she'd met the kids at Philosophy Club, she'd gotten in the habit of locking the dumb, everyday world out when one of her exciting new friends wasn't around. Nobody else mattered enough to catch her interest. Nobody and nothing.

Mom was practically breathing fire. "Annie, when you quit going to church last month I tried to reason with you but left the decision up to you. I've been trying to trust you. But the school called today, Annie. You've been cutting class! Where are you going? Annie, answer me! What's going on with you?"

Ann wished Mom would mind her own business. But on the other hand, there was still a part of her, deep inside, that wished she had a little guidance. Her new friends were exciting, but they called the shots and she just went along, afraid to say no. And sometimes she wondered how far she could go with a crowd like that without suddenly being in over her head.

## What would you do?

*If she talks to Mom about what's going on, turn to page 102.*
*If she angrily shuts her out, turn to page 83.*

"Just go away and leave me alone!" Ann yelled. "It's my life, and I'm living it the way I want, so butt out!"

"Annie!" Mom yelled. But then a tear formed on her cheek. "Why won't you talk to me like you used to? Or if you can't talk to me, why don't you come back to your friends at church and talk to them?"

Mom was really crying now, and Ann took advantage of that weakness by charging into the bathroom, slamming the door and bolting the lock. The next day she moved into the big apartment rented by several kids from the Philosophy Club. She started dealing a little dope around school to pay her part of the expenses, and by the end of the month she'd cut her ties with home completely.

Things were exciting and fun in the new apartment— everybody drifted in and out all day and night. Of course, her grades plummetted, and she dropped out of school in November of her senior year. That was okay, though, because everybody in her crowd knew that a high school education was a bust anyway. They never taught anything of real value. And Ann could make good money dealing—more than any job that required a high school diploma.

■

She was 22 when the accident happened. Nicky and a friend of his were trying to put a TV antenna on the old house Nicky was renting, and they were both electrocuted when the antenna hit a power line. Nicky, of course, was stoned at the time. Ann knew that's why he'd been careless, and her whole world crashed down on her.

For three weeks she lay on her pallet in the apartment, drinking non-stop and smoking whatever was around. Then, she blacked out a few times when she tried to get up and find food. That scared her, so much that she panicked and called home. It was the only place she could turn. Her friends were too stoned to help her and wouldn't have known how to help anyway.

"Mom? It's me."

That's all she could say. Why she suddenly felt tight all over, like she was about to shatter and fall into pieces, she didn't know. It took her by surprise and so did the tears that crowded behind her eyes.

"Oh, Annie," Mom said eagerly. "What do you need?"

Ann could only choke out one word, but it was enough to make Mom come running to help. It was enough to open the door so Mom could bring her home and help her heal.

"You," she said.

The End

"Oh, Tara, I'm so sorry," she murmured, then swallowed hard and looked straight ahead. Stupid! Stupid! Stupid! hammered through her brain. Say something comforting to her! Be a friend to her! But she was even afraid to glance over at Tara, though she could hear occasional sniffles that told her Tara was still crying.

"You know," Tara whispered at one point. "Sometimes, well, sometimes I feel so depressed I almost ... almost want to just end things. Just want to take some pills or jump in the pool and drown or something to be with Jillian."

Ann felt numb and her heart slammed. But she couldn't think of anything appropriate to say to such a horrifying confession. As soon as she could, Ann made some feeble excuse and left. The rest of the day, she wondered how she should've handled the situation. How would somebody else with more self-confidence have responded to Tara when she told about her sister and about her own suicidal thoughts?

The next night at the youth group meeting, the kids were talking about Jeff Harrison, the center on the Crestview basketball team whose father had just died of emphysema.

"It's rough for him and his sisters right now," Randy, a good friend of Jeff's, told the group. "They're taking it pretty hard—well, I guess any of us would."

There were quiet nods around the circle, and Ann's throat felt tight. "So Randy? How do you ... talk to him?" she blurted. "How do you make yourself go over there and talk to him?"

She immediately felt flustered—boy, that sounded like a stupid thing to ask. But Randy didn't take it that way.

"It's hard, Ann," he said solemnly. "Half the time I don't know what to say. I think, though, it's important just to be there for them. To listen more than anything."

She took a deep breath. "See, yesterday Tara Hastings told me ... she told me I reminded her of her sister who was killed six months ago. And I felt so ... "

"... overwhelmed?" Randy finished the sentence Ann couldn't find words to finish herself. "Helpless?"

Ann nodded, her eyes burning. "I didn't know how to react. I felt really uncomfortable."

"Let her open up to you, Ann," Chris, the youth minister, added. "She needs someone now, and she's chosen you. Don't turn your back."

Ann knew he was right, but still she wondered if she could get up the nerve to reach out to someone in Tara's kind of pain.

---

## What would you do?

*If Ann makes a real effort to get to know Tara, turn to page 118.*
*If she can't bring herself to reach out, turn to page 128.*

Tara laughed. "Not so fast, Ann! That kind of commitment's too much for me, you know? But I may drop into church, just visiting, once in a while."

"Sure," Ann said, a little embarrassed. "Any time. If you need a ride, call me."

Tara did come to church a couple of times, but she seemed restless. She doodled on the back of her bulletin during the sermon and whispered to Ann so much that Ann started feeling like everyone in the church could hear them.

And then Tara started running around with the popular crowd at school—Hillary Stanton and her friends. Hillary's friends thought church was boring, so Tara stopped attending.

She still waved to Ann in the halls at school, though, and talked to her whenever she could. And then one day, Hillary herself came up to Ann as she stuffed her books in her locker.

"So, Tara tells us you're pretty cool, Ann." Hillary's voice was husky, lots of kids said "sexy." "Want to come to a party at my place this Sunday night? Tara said she'd pick you up."

Ann was stunned. The popular girls were actually considering *her* as friend material. But she had youth group Sunday night. Was the party a good enough reason to miss?

## What would you do?

*If Ann goes to Hillary's party, turn to page 63.*
*If she decides to pass, turn to page 72.*

Ann decided to ignore the gossip, but still it took its toll on her. Her nerves became raw from wondering who was whispering what behind her back. She thought about trying to at least set the record straight with the kids in her youth group, but she couldn't get up the nerve. What if they wouldn't believe her? What if they, too, were convinced she'd stolen that jewelry? The censure of everybody at school was bad enough, but she couldn't face all the shame if even her Christian friends stayed convinced she was a thief. So she wordlessly withdrew further into herself and avoided everybody completely, feeling practically too self-conscious to function at all.

By the time the rumors died down, she'd formed a defensive habit of staying totally alone. Then one afternoon she was in an isolated spot in a corner of the library, when Desiree Snyder came up and sat across from her.

"There's bad karma here," Desiree whispered, her shoulder-length earrings clattering as she shook her head worriedly. "You're giving off disturbing vibrations, Ann. Vibrations of tension and despair. I can help, if you let me."

Desiree and her crowd were different from the other juniors at Crestview High, and everyone pretty much avoided them. Most of them were into art or music, and several of them made the highest grades in off-beat classes like contemporary poetry and oriental mythologies. Desiree had skin so pale she seemed made of porcelain. She dressed mostly in black and was, to say the least, striking. She'd never spoken to Ann before.

"How?" Ann asked, swallowing hard. It was true she was feeling miserable these days. "What do you mean?"

"By opening the channels of your creativity. Come to a meeting tonight. Let your soul breathe."

She drifted away like a puff of smoke, and Ann stared at the address on the slip of paper Desiree had left lying on the table.

■

Ann timidly knocked on the door at 501 Hamilton, an upstairs apartment near the college. It was opened by a boy with a ponytail and one dangling earring who silently led her into a room where a couple of dozen kids were seated on pillows around a cluster of burning white candles.

There was a discussion going on, something about

imagination. As Ann's eyes became accustomed to the dim light, she recognized several kids from Desiree's crowd. The others looked older, like college students. Some of the people held wine glasses. A haze of sweet-smelling smoke hung over the circle.

"We have to constantly see and evaluate life with the eyes of a child," a thin young man with a black beard was saying. "Philosophers, such as Jesus Christ, have long known this to be true. That's why Christ said the kingdom of heaven belonged to the children. The kingdom of heaven isn't some mythic place in the clouds but is right here on Earth, today, for anyone with imagination enough to see it!"

That sounded a little off to Ann, and the marijuana smoke was beginning to bother her. She was beginning to feel a little hazy, like a spell was falling over her. She wondered whether to resist or just let it happen.

## What would you do?

*If Ann resists, turn to page 119.*
*If she lets it sweep over her, turn to page 81.*

Ann forced herself to act upbeat when she gave Janene her going-away present three weeks later, and she waved exuberantly as her parents' car turned the corner and went out of sight. But that night, alone in her room, she couldn't stop thinking of how far away Janene was, and she cried herself to sleep.

The next morning, Sunday, she woke red-eyed and miserable, and considered skipping church to stay home and brood a little more. But Mom wouldn't hear of it.

"Come on, Annie, it'll do you good to be around the kids," she said softly. "It'll get your mind off your problems, and who knows? This may be the very day you'll make a new friend."

"Fat chance," Ann muttered, going grumpily into the shower.

But a couple of hours later, Rachelle Washington unexpectedly sat down next to Ann and Mom in the sanctuary.

"Did Janene leave this weekend?" she whispered.

Ann bit her lip, looked at her hands and nodded.

To Ann's surprise, Rachelle squeezed her shoulder.

"Hey, why don't you come and sit with us?" She gestured toward where some of the other senior high kids shared a pew near the back of the church. Ann had been too shy to sit there with them before Janene, and since Janene she hadn't had to. She and Janene had always sat together beside Mom.

The sad cloud in her head lifted a little at Rachelle's offer. Was it possible they wanted to be her friend?

No, probably they just felt sorry for her. Or maybe it was only Rachelle, and not even the others, who had the idea of inviting her. In fact, maybe the others would even object or snicker if she came over. That would be so humiliating.

"I don't think so ..." she murmured, looking away.

"Oh." Rachelle hesitated a second. "Well, okay."

Ann felt her get up and leave, and tears throbbed in her throat. Why did things have to be like this? Why did she have to imagine the worst all the time? What if ... what if the kids really did want her back there, in their pew?

Maybe it was time she got enough confidence to trust herself and to trust other people not to deliberately hurt her.

She got up all her courage and peeked over her shoulder. Everyone on the high school pew was looking toward her. No one was snickering. They looked ... what? Concerned? Even disappointed, maybe?

"Mom, I'll see you later, okay?" She stood quickly, before she could chicken out, and turned and walked back to the senior high pew.

"Can I squeeze in?" she whispered, her heart beating in her throat.

Seven bright smiles greeted her, and seven people eagerly scooted over to make more room.

"We're really glad to have you here," Rachelle beamed. "We're just starting to plan a party, and we can use your brain power."

"Not just 'a' party," Randy Miller amended, leaning toward Ann. " 'The' party. This party will be excellent! We're gonna invite all the kids in town. Kind of a way of reaching out, you know? Showing everybody how much fun you can have without beer and drugs and stuff like that."

At that moment, the organist began to play and they quieted down. But that night at youth group, the planning began in earnest.

Ann was thrilled to be a part of the action and eagerly helped take care of decorations and publicity over the next three weeks. By party night, the church fellowship hall had transformed, with a sound system monopolizing one wall and food tables stretching along another. Three pingpong tables were huddled in one section of the room, and Randy even had the great idea of renting a big-screen television and setting it up in the lobby.

"What if nobody shows up after all our work and planning?" Cora Bagis asked that evening, worriedly gnawing a thumbnail.

---

## Blind choice:

*Without looking ahead, turn to page 101 or page 117 to continue the story.*

Traci was leaning against the coffee machine in the waiting room of the intensive care unit, looking stunned. Ann rushed up and, without a word, put her arms around her. The moment she did it she realized Traci might angrily push her away, because of what she'd told Traci's mother on the phone.

But Traci put her head on Ann's shoulder and sobbed.

"Oh, thank goodness you came," she whispered. "Mom's in there with Dad. He's in awful shape, Ann. He may ... may die."

Ann, crying too, wordlessly rocked her friend like a baby and let Traci release as much of her fear and panic as she could.

"Don't leave, okay Ann? Stay here?"

"Sure, you know I will," Ann said. "And Trace? Whatever happens—I'll be here for you, no matter what."

Traci nodded weakly. "You know, Dad's in a coma now. But I got here in time to ... to talk to him a little ... before. Thanks for telling Mom where I was."

"You're welcome," Ann whispered, and a strange thing occurred to her then. She decided that the truth was often most important when it was most difficult to tell—particularly to a friend.

Traci's dad stayed in the hospital for several more weeks after he came out of his coma. During that time, Ann and her mom brought food to the Chandler's house and just kept them company when they could. Ann and Traci still enjoyed their friendship, but the petty games they'd played before just didn't seem to matter now. The shock of Traci's dad's accident helped them see that life is too important to treat it like a game. And honesty is too vital to healthy relationships to ever lie to each other—or their families—again.

The End

After lots of soul-searching, Ann finally decided she just wasn't strong enough to stand up to Tara when she had to, and so their friendship was doomed. It would've been wonderful if she could've influenced Tara for the better and maybe even helped convince her to become a Christian. But Ann knew she might as well face facts—Tara had the stronger personality. It was she who'd gradually bend Ann to her will—not the other way around.

So Ann stayed pretty much a loner 'til one day in May when she was assigned a team book report in English with Desiree Snyder. Desiree was known as a free spirit around the school, one of the small group of kids who were into art, music and philosophy. Ann, like many of the other juniors at Crestview High, was a little intimidated by Desiree and at the same time admired her. She was striking, in an off-beat way, with her pale skin, mostly black outfits and long earrings. She was never afraid to speak her mind and did just that to Ann one day in the library.

"You know, Ann, I've been fascinated by you for a long time. I sense layers of consciousness in you that you've barely begun to tap," she whispered.

Ann, taken by surprise and flattered that Desiree had noticed her at all, could only stammer, "Really?"

Desiree squinted thoughtfully into her eyes and nodded.

"Come with me, Ann. To a meeting. There's a club some of us belong to—a Philosophy Club. We talk about some fascinating things—New-Age ideas, music, art. Just being there will open channels of your creativity you probably don't dream you have."

"Oh, I don't think so," Ann murmured.

"Don't 'think.' Come. I'll pick you up tonight at 9:00." Desiree smiled as though that settled things, and Ann felt herself smile back. After all, it wasn't like her social calendar was too packed to go to a little meeting. And it was nice of Desiree to single her out to invite.

■

When they knocked at the door of 501 Hamilton, an apartment near the college campus, it was opened by a guy with a ponytail and one dangling earring who silently led them into a room where a couple of dozen kids were seated on pillows around a cluster of burning white candles.

There was a discussion going on, something about

imagination. As Ann's eyes became accustomed to the dim light, she recognized several kids from Desiree's crowd. The others looked older, like college students. Some of the people held wine glasses. A haze of sweet-smelling marijuana smoke hung over the circle.

Ann had been listening quietly for maybe half an hour when a thin young man with a black beard spoke.

"We have to constantly see and evaluate life with the eyes of a child," he said. "Philosophers, such as Jesus Christ, have always known this to be true. That's why Christ said the kingdom of heaven belonged to the children. The kingdom of heaven isn't some mythic place in the clouds, but is right here on Earth for anyone with imagination enough to see it!"

The discussion suddenly seemed heady and a little confusing to Ann. And the marijuana smoke was starting to bother her. She felt something like a spell slowly falling over her, and wondered whether to resist or let it happen.

## What would you do?

*If she resists, turn to page 119.*
*If she lets it sweep over her, turn to page 81.*

"Rachelle, you wouldn't believe where I've been today," Ann heard herself begin. Then she described the opulence of Tara's house and repeated the information Tara had confided about her parents and their obsessive work patterns. The casually offered wine cooler, even Tara's expensive clothing and the way she nonchalantly tossed around her shiny hair—every detail was in there, poured from Ann's mouth to Rachelle's ear.

"Ann ... I can't believe it," Rachelle sounded awed when Ann finally finished. "I mean, I definitely noticed Tara at school last week. Who could not notice somebody that looks like her? But I didn't dream she had so many problems."

"Uh, well, I didn't exactly mean she had problems," Ann interjected weakly.

But Rachelle brushed that off.

"Listen, I've got to go. I've got a couple of other people I want to call, but I'll see you at church tomorrow, okay? Remember to sit with us in the sanctuary. Bye."

Usually, Ann sat with Mom in the sanctuary, too self-conscious to sit with the other kids in "their" pew. She smiled at the direct invitation, but a little twinge of worry caught at the back of her mind. Would Rachelle tell the other people she called about Tara? Ann felt remorse at the thought.

But Rachelle was a strong Christian, and she and the other youth group kids would just want to help Tara. So it had surely been good to tell the story honestly.

■

By the next morning, every teenager in Hilltop Church seemed to know every detail of Tara Hasting's life. And what they didn't know, they were eager to learn from Ann. For the first time ever, she found herself the center of a crowd of people, the attention focused on her. And she liked the feeling—a lot.

"So, this pool at Tara's house," Randy Miller slipped in next to Ann as they were all gathered in the church lobby between Sunday school and worship service. "Does she have, you know, major wild parties out there?"

"Oh, I'll bet," Ann said, laughing a little. "They sure have their refrigerator well-stocked with liquid refreshments, if you know what I mean."

Things were even better at youth group that night. Rachelle

and Keri Jones drove by to pick up Ann (a first), and probed for more details of what Keri was starting to call The Mansion.

"So Tara has this whole place to herself?" Keri asked.

"Yeah, pretty much. She says her parents live at their offices," Ann answered, amazed at how confident she felt now that she had a hot topic to talk about and people eager to hear.

■

At school the next morning, Rachelle and Keri went out of their way again to hang around Ann and asked her to join their table in the cafeteria at lunch. There, they encouraged her to tell some details of her day with Tara to the kids who hadn't already heard. Ann felt flustered but flattered and talked a little. That warm feeling of being the focus of attention took hold of her, and she found herself breaking through her shyness to elaborate and make what she was telling funny and exciting. She felt, for the first time, like a confident, accepted member of the crowd around her.

After school, she saw Tara alone by her locker. Tara turned her head and stared right at her, right through her. She knew. About the talking Ann had done, the stories she'd told over and over the past two days.

From the look in her eyes, Ann was positive. Tara knew.

That look made Ann feel sort of sick. She figured maybe she should apologize, but then again, apologize for what? For just telling about her day with Tara exactly as it had happened?

## What would you do?

*If Ann apologizes to Tara, turn to page 31.*
*If she doesn't see a need to, turn to page 109.*

Suddenly, panic overtook her, along with the icy truth.

Hillary and Tara and the others won't understand what I'm feeling! She recognized how pathetic but true that sounded the moment she thought it. They only want friends who're having fun and being fun. They don't want to mess with heavy things like ... like this hurt inside me.

It was hard owning up to that. So hard that she put her head in her hands and prayed out loud.

"I don't know what to do, Lord! I feel so ... alone. Help me, please!"

Almost at that exact moment, a loud clattering wheeze sounded just outside her window. She jerked her head up in surprise, and saw five of the youth group kids scrambling out of Randy Miller's old beat-up Jeep.

"... you're not alone ... not alone ..." went through her mind, through her heart. Was God whispering to her? Or was her own joy at the sight of the kids coming up her sidewalk reminding her of something she'd almost forgotten? No, the kids from church wouldn't ever give up on her, no matter how rude she'd been, no matter how neglectful. They were with her always, just as Jesus had promised he would be. She knew that, deep inside, and it felt so good she wanted to shout for joy.

Instead, she scrambled to her feet and hurried to open the front door for them.

"Uh, hi Ann," Cora Bagis said, smiling a little tentatively, as though unsure of her welcome. "We heard about your father, and, well, we hope you won't feel like we're intruding, but we wanted you to know we're thinking about you."

"If you want to talk or anything, we're here to listen," Jason Kyle added softly.

"Thanks, Lord," Ann prayed silently, then she took a deep, relieved breath.

"Come in, please," she said, throwing the door wide open. "I've ... I've missed you all so much."

The End

"Wow, that'd be great!" Ann responded.

■

Mom, however, wasn't quite that thrilled.

"Have you met Tara's parents?" Mom asked impatiently.

"No, Mom, but they sound fine. And Tara says there'll be gobs of other adults around. Her mother's having a big party."

"What about church? And youth group?"

"It won't kill me to miss, just once."

A little reluctantly, Mom said okay, and the girls drove to the lake Saturday afternoon in Tara's red Mustang convertible.

Tara's lake house turned out to be a spectacular three-level mansion on the water's edge. It was alive with people and music when they arrived. Tara's mother welcomed them from behind the bar on the broad patio facing the water. Her father absently waved his glass toward them from his place beside a young woman near the piano.

"Sorry, he's preoccupied, darling," Mrs. Hastings explained to Tara. "Leave it to your father to pick the most attractive and youngest guest to entertain."

The bitterness in Mrs. Hastings' voice made Ann uncomfortable, but Tara drug her away to her room and they changed into their swimsuits.

Ann saw little of Tara's parents the rest of the weekend, since she and Tara spent most of their time on the lake shore. But the loud music and laughter were always a reminder that the party was still going strong up at the house.

It turned out that Tara had invited her new boyfriend, Roger Hartley, and his best friend, Tim Jenkins, to drive down for a few hours Sunday. The four teenagers spent the afternoon in the boat, with a couple of six-packs and a radio for company. The plan had been to water-ski around the lake, but after the guys had their first beer, they quickly forgot about anything involving that much exertion and concentration.

Instead, Roger and Tara lazed in each other's arms, and Tim and Ann talked, swam a little and just soaked up rays until sunset.

■

"Well, did you have fun?" Tara asked.

The wind whipped their still-damp hair as they drove back to

Crestview that night with the top down.

"Sure," Ann yelled to be heard.

And she really did. Of course, she'd also felt uncomfortable some of the time, and a little afraid too.

"Next week, we'll have even more fun!" Tara smiled mysteriously. "I've got a surprise planned."

■

Mom was waiting up for Ann, smiling with interest. "Well, did you have a nice weekend?"

A "nice" weekend? Ann wondered if Mom could handle even hearing about the kind of party the Hastings threw! If she mentioned the boys or the booze, she could forget about getting permission to go again next week. Still, she'd never lied to Mom before, and Mom was always good at helping her sort things through. Should she level with her or brush off her questions?

## What would you do?

*If Ann tells Mom honestly about her weekend, turn to page 131.*
*If she brushes her off instead, turn to page 127.*

"Uh, I don't think we have to worry about that," said Jason Kyle, pointing to a stream of cars pulling into the church parking lot.

An hour or so later, when things had been going strong for a while, Tara found Ann and yelled in her ear to be heard above the music and laughter.

"This is some of the most fun I've ever had sober!"

Ann gave her a sideways look and smiled but shook her head.

"Okay, okay!" Tara laughed. "This is some of the most fun I've ever had period. Everybody's having fun."

Ann felt her mouth stretch into a wider grin. She looked out over all the kids. Old friends, friends-to-be. This was so much better than brooding alone in her room or trying to fit where she didn't belong.

"I'm really glad you came," Ann told Tara sincerely. "And Tara? I hope you'll come back."

The End

"Nothing, all right? Nothing's going on with me, except that I'm living my own life and having a good time. You know what your problem is, Mom? You don't care about my friends. You've never taken the trouble to get to know them, but still you've just decided to hate them for no reason. You have no right to judge them!"

"I don't hate your friends, Annie," Mom said quietly. "You're right—I hardly know them. They won't come in and visit. They just wait in their cars for you, smoking, looking bored. Or they bring you home and you practically stumble going up the stairs to your room. Annie, do you think I'm deaf, dumb and blind? I know you're . . . you're using either drugs or alcohol or both. No, I don't hate your friends, Annie. I just hate the person you've become because of them."

Ann sat down miserably on the edge of her bed. She thought she'd built enough walls around herself to block all feeling, but that last sentence got through to her. Mom hated the person she was now. That hurt.

"Listen," Ann said, running a nail-bitten hand through her close-cropped hair. "I don't think you understand what I'm into these days. See, I'm just exploring. The Philosophy Club encourages people to constantly challenge their beliefs and their lifestyles. I'm just experimenting, trying to find the real me."

"But Annie, it's one thing to discuss a lot of different ways of thinking. But it's something else to lose your own sense of direction and to no longer know what you believe. Or who you trust. Who do you trust now, Annie? It's obviously not me or your old friends at church. Do you even trust God any longer? And can you trust these new friends of yours?"

Ann threw herself backward onto the bed and stared at the ceiling. After a couple of minutes, Mom went out, closing the door quietly behind her.

■

A few days later, Desiree grabbed Ann and pulled her into the restroom at school. When she'd checked to be sure they were alone, she smiled broadly and took a tiny packet of white powder from the inside pocket of her jacket.

"Nicky gave me this for you, Ann. An early birthday present. If you think marijuana makes you fly, wait 'til you try cocaine."

Ann's breath froze in her throat. She raised a hand and touched the tiny, innocent-looking packet, then recoiled as though it'd been a rattlesnake.

"I can't, Des," she said. Then took a deep breath. "I mean, I don't want to. It's not for me. Sorry."

Desiree looked stunned for a second, then angry.

"Listen, think for a minute. How do you think Nicky and some of the others make their rent? Nicky's parents kicked him out years ago, and to keep his apartment he has to deal. But he's giving this to you, don't you see? How do you think he's going to feel if you turn down his gift?"

Ann swallowed hard. "I understand," she whispered. "But I can't. It's not for me."

Desiree walked away, and Ann wondered if she'd seen the last of her. She also knew if she hadn't been challenged by Mom the other night, she might've tried the cocaine. But who, really, did she trust?

"I trust you, God," she whispered, looking at the scared, lonely person in the mirror. "I'm ready to listen again. Set me straight, okay?"

From the feeling of sudden peace and strength that came over her, Ann knew he'd heard her prayer.

The End

But as Ann opened her mouth to unload the juicy details of Tara's lifestyle, Mrs. Hogelman's voice slipped quietly into her brain. Mrs. Hogelman, Ann's kindergarten Sunday school teacher, had repeatedly told her class to "do to others what you would have them do to you." Even after over 10 years, Ann often found that Bible verse ringing in her head at times like this. Ann couldn't imagine anything she'd like less than someone gossiping about her over the phone. And what she'd like most was to be invited to more parties and things—and maybe Tara felt that way too.

"Rachelle, do you think it'd be okay if I brought a guest to the movie party the youth group is planning for next week?"

"Sure. Who's the guest?"

"Oh, just someone who needs her taste in movies changed," Ann said with a grin. "A new friend of mine."

"Oh," Rachelle said slyly. "Does that mean you've given up on Jason asking you to go with him to the party?"

Ann felt her neck burn. Why, why, why had she confided to Rachelle that she had a crush on Jason Kyle?

"Oh, him," she murmured. "I've given up on him totally." Ann hoped she sounded convincing.

"Sure you have!" Rachelle laughed. "See you tomorrow."

It took Ann a few minutes to shove Jason far enough back in her mind so she could dial Tara's number. Every time she thought of the way his gray eyes crinkled at the corners when he laughed and of the habit he had of pushing his light brown hair back from his face when he was in a serious discussion, she felt herself go a little weak. She just wished she could figure out—was that real interest she felt coming from him when he'd lean toward her and listen so closely to the few things she could get nerve enough to contribute in youth group? Or was he just feeling sorry for her because she was so shy and trying to help her along?

She shivered hard to drive those eyes out of her mind and dialed Tara's number.

■

Tara was delighted to be asked to the party. As they drove in Ann's Volkswagen Rabbit to meet the kids at Crestview Cinema, Ann was really glad she'd asked her.

In fact, Tara fit in great with the other kids. By the time the movie had ended and they were all at Taco Casa, she was laughing and telling silly jokes as though she'd been part of the group forever.

But right about then—between rounds of tacos—Jason Kyle got out of his chair beside Ann, drug it over and pulled it into the skinny space beside Tara. He draped an arm loosely over the back of her chair. Tara turned to him, looked in his eyes and briefly touched his dangling hand. And from that moment, her witty comments and funny stories were directed to him alone.

Through burning eyes, Ann saw it all.

Here she had gone far out of her way to include Tara, and this was the way Tara repaid her for her friendship! Tara had stolen her boyfriend and didn't even care!

## What would you do?

*If Ann angrily confronts Tara about Jason, turn to page 56.*
*If Ann is hurt and snubs Tara from then on, turn to page 65.*

"I'd like to know more about her, if you'd like to tell me," Ann said softly. Tara nodded, smiling through her tears. They settled back on the sofa.

And then Ann listened for over an hour while Tara talked of the pain she'd felt, and was still feeling, over Jillian's death. Though Ann wondered if she was helping at all, Tara seemed to crave just the kind of quiet support Ann offered.

In fact, over the next weeks a strong bond formed between the two girls, and both knew the confidences Tara continued to share with Ann about Jillian were one reason for that bond.

"Come with me to our lake house next weekend," Tara said one May morning when they were walking to history together. "My parents are having a party out there. If it's warm enough, we can take the boat out and water-ski."

"Oh, Tara, I don't know," Ann began slowly. "I have church and stuff Sunday."

"Oh, please, Ann? I've been so lonely at my folks' parties since Jillian ... please?"

When she put it that way, how could a real friend refuse? "And Roger and Tim may drop by the lake for a while too," Tara added, leaning close to Ann's ear and smiling slyly.

Roger Hartley and Tara had been dating a lot recently, and Tim Jenkins, Roger's best friend, was a guy Tara knew Ann had a crush on. The idea of spending some time alone with him and Roger and Tara at the lake was exciting—and scary too. But Ann overruled her fears—surely the party would be well-chaperoned.

Still, when Ann asked for Mom's permission to go to the lake that weekend, she decided not to mention the boys.

■

Tara's lake house turned out to be a spectacular sprawling mansion built on three levels at the water's edge. As they drove up, a crowd of people was milling around the bar and tables on the patio, and music filtered through the air.

"My parents and their friends," Tara muttered with a sigh. "We'll say 'hi' and then take off on our own, okay?"

"Darlings!" A tall, elegant woman who looked exactly like an older version of Tara came quickly across the lawn, a drink in her hand. She kissed Tara on the cheek, then pointed to where two tall, dark-haired boys were sunbathing on the private beach below the house. "Sweetheart, your adorable beau and his friend arrived an hour ago. I helped them make themselves at home. They've got the boat all stocked, and they're waiting for you two."

"Oh, thanks, Mom," Tara said quickly, then bent to grab her swimsuit and Ann's from the back of the convertible. She threw Ann's toward her and took off running for the beach. "Come on, slow poke!" she yelled, laughing, over her shoulder.

■

Half an hour later, Tim, Roger, Tara and Ann were miles from land, raiding the well-stocked small refrigerator in the boat's hold. Tara had skied, and it was Ann's turn next. But first, Tim popped the tops off beers and passed them around.

"No thanks," Ann shrugged and asked for a Coke instead.

But Tara took the offered beer and the next one too. After half an hour, all thoughts of letting Ann ski had evaporated. Roger stretched in the bottom of the boat, Tara's head across his chest. Tim draped an arm across Ann's shoulders.

"Let's go to The Cove!" Tim called down to Roger.

Tara nodded excitedly in agreement. And Roger got up and, hugging Tara close with one hand, steered toward a lighted shore.

■

The Cove turned out to be a club at the lake's edge, a place you could only reach by water.

"Won't they card us?" Ann asked worriedly.

"Nah." Tara threw a T-shirt over her bikini. "My parents are members here, and they don't card the members' kids."

They entered the dark building without being stopped, and soon Tara and Roger were swaying on the dance floor to the slow, seductive music. Tim pulled Ann out of the booth they'd shared and pulled her close to him too.

After half an hour, Tara laughingly pried Ann loose from Tim and drug her into the restroom for a conference.

"This is going so great!" she breathed, studying herself in the mirror and wiping off a smudge of mascara. "My folks and their friends will be going into town dancing 'til the middle of the night, so we'll have the house to ourselves!"

She winked in the mirror at Ann. "Roger and I have dibs on the master bedroom."

Suddenly, Ann felt used. She'd come here this weekend mostly because Tara said she needed her to get over the painful memories of Jillian. But now, Ann wondered if she was just a convenient date for Tim, so Tara could have Roger here.

Of course on the other hand, what was so bad about that? Tim was cute. That was for sure.

## What would you do?

*If Ann goes along with Tara's plan for the night, turn to page 44.*
*If she tries to set the record straight instead, turn to page 58.*

Tara abruptly turned her back on Ann and slammed her locker shut. Ann reluctantly went over to her.

"Tara, I ..."

"I liked you, Ann," Tara broke in, whirling back around with tears in her eyes. "How could you have talked about me to everybody like that? I hate you now. I really do. Stay away from me, and never try to talk to me again. Understand?"

Ann watched, stunned, as Tara ran angrily down the hall and out the school. Then she sank against the lockers and slid to sit on the floor. She couldn't breathe, and the walls were closing in on her. Tara had probably been right—she was worthless. There was no explanation for her and her behavior. No wonder nobody really liked her. She was really, really pathetic.

She made a decision then and there not to inflict herself on anybody again. The decision wasn't that hard to make, since she couldn't face talking to people anyway. Especially the kids in the youth group, now that she'd run her mouth off so sickeningly.

Over the next weeks, she sullenly rejected all their attempts to draw her back into the life of the church and shut herself off into an invisible cocoon of loneliness and depression.

■

One day, when she was in her usual isolated spot in a far corner of the library, Desiree Snyder came up and sat across from her.

"There's bad karma here," Desiree whispered, her shoulder-length earrings clattering as she shook her head worriedly. "You're giving off disturbing vibrations, Ann. Vibrations of tension and despair. I can help, if you let me."

Desiree and her crowd were different from the other juniors at Crestview High. Most everyone respected them but tended to just leave them alone. Desiree's friends were into art or music, and several of them made the highest grades in off-beat classes like contemporary poetry and oriental mythologies. Desiree had skin so pale she seemed made of porcelain. She dressed mostly in black and was, to say the least, striking. She'd never spoken to Ann before.

"How?" Ann asked, swallowing hard. It was true she was feeling miserable these days. "What do you mean?"

"Come to a meeting tonight, Ann. Let your soul breathe."

Desiree drifted away like a puff of smoke, and Ann stared at the address on the slip of paper Desiree had left lying on the table.

■

Ann timidly knocked on the door at 501 Hamilton, an up-stairs apartment near the college. It was opened by a guy with a ponytail and one dangling earring who silently led her into a room where a couple of dozen kids were seated on pillows around a cluster of burning white candles.

There was a discussion going on, something about imagination. As Ann's eyes became accustomed to the dim light, she recognized several kids from Desiree's crowd. The others looked older, like college students. Some of the people held wine glasses. A haze of sweet-smelling marijuana smoke hung over the circle.

She sat down quietly in the circle and tried to understand what the others were discussing. After a while, a thin young man with a black beard spoke.

"We have to constantly see and evaluate life with the eyes of a child," he was saying. "Philosophers, such as Jesus Christ, have long known this to be true. That's why Christ said the kingdom of heaven belonged to the children. The kingdom of heaven isn't some mythic place in the clouds but is right here on Earth, today, for anyone with imagination enough to see it!"

The conversation suddenly seemed heady and a little confusing to Ann. And the marijuana smoke was beginning to bother her. She slowly felt something like a spell falling over her, and wondered whether to resist or let it happen.

---

## What would you do?

*If Ann resists, turn to page 119.*
*If she lets it sweep over her, turn to page 81.*

Ann was stunned. "I ... can't do that, Trace."

"What do you mean you can't?" Traci sounded truly puzzled. "I told you exactly what to say. Trust me—it'll work perfectly."

"Sorry, but I just can't tell a bald-faced lie that way."

"Oh," Traci's voice was cool. No, cold. "Fine, then—friend."

The click on Traci's end of the line sounded final to Ann, and sure enough, it was. Over the next number of weeks, Traci shunned Ann completely. And she'd obviously turned the other girls against Ann too. They looked at her now in the same ridiculing way they had all looked at Hillary's gang before.

And then one night, Janene called.

"How've you been, Ann?" she asked nervously. "I haven't seen you much lately."

Ann's throat burned. "That's not my fault," she forced out. "I'm right at school where I've always been, in plain sight. You guys are just ... avoiding me."

There were a few seconds of silence on the line, then Janene's voice sounded a little shaky.

"I know, Ann. Traci wanted everyone to ignore you, but I think she's wrong. They all are. I ... want to be friends still, no matter what Traci says."

"Wow, Janene, I want that too," Ann choked out.

Over the next weeks, Janene and Ann became closer and closer. Ann had never imagined how wonderful it could feel to have a friend she could trust with her deepest thoughts and dreams like she trusted Janene. Or to have someone to share a joke with or a hot fudge sundae or even to cry with at sad movies. She and Janene thought they'd be best friends forever.

And then Janene's father was transferred.

"We're moving in three weeks," Janene told Ann over the phone. "Oh, Ann, I'm going to miss you so much!"

Ann was nearly overwhelmed with sadness and loss. Janene was the one truly close friend she'd ever had, and she didn't know if she could make other friends. Should she even try? Or should she pull in and keep her pain and loneliness tight inside?

## What would you do?

*If Ann reaches out to another group of kids, turn to page 90.*
*If she decides to go it alone, turn to page 33.*

Without a word, so flustered her face was burning, Ann slipped out the door and went quickly home.

She stayed awake late that night, watching the stars out her bedroom window and thinking. Why was it that all the activities in town relied on booze or dope or sex—or all three—for fun?

The next Sunday night, she asked that same question to the other members of her youth group.

Randy Miller shrugged. "I guess nobody wants to take the time to try to plan anything better."

"It would be nice if somebody did, though," Rachelle said quickly, giving Ann a wistful look. "The crowd I run around with used to be into things I really enjoyed—biking, picnics, things like that. But lately, the parties I'm invited to get wilder and wilder."

"Maybe *we* should provide an alternative," Ann heard herself suggest, her heart pounding. "We've got a huge fellowship hall. We could probably find a Christian rock group we could ask to play, and use tapes the rest of the time. And we're *great* at planning food."

The others laughed, and a buzz of planning began to grow among the kids.

"But hold on a second, before everybody gets too excited," said level-headed Robert Longton. "Reverend Sumner and the church board would have to okay it, and they probably wouldn't go for the idea."

"Only one way to find out." Cora Bagis jumped to her feet. "Who's coming with me to ask?"

■

"I've thought for a long time that the fellowship hall was the perfect place for a big community youth bash." Reverend Sumner's eyes flashed enthusiastically. "We'll even empty ice from the church ice-maker into plastic bags for a week ahead of time so you kids will have all the cubes you need for your soft drinks."

"All right!" Randy laughed and clapped his hands, then gave Ann a high-five.

■

Ann was thrilled to be a part of the action, and eagerly helped decorate and publicize the party over the next three weeks. By party night, the church fellowship hall had been transformed. A sound system monopolized one wall and food tables another. Three pingpong tables were set up in one area of the room, and Randy even had the great idea of renting a big-screen television and setting it up in the lobby.

"What if nobody shows up?" Cora asked that evening, worriedly gnawing a thumbnail.

## Blind choice:

*Without looking ahead, turn to page 101 or page 117 to continue the story.*

"What are *you* doing here?" Traci snapped when Ann walked into the waiting room of the intensive care unit at Mercy.

Ann just stood miserably staring at Traci, slumped in an orange plastic chair. She looked white and shaken.

"Where's your mother? And where's ... Todd?" Ann whispered.

"Mom's in there, with Dad. And do you really think Todd would show his face in here, after you blabbed to my mother about us? She'll probably never speak to him again, and maybe not to me either. And it's your fault, Ann."

"I just ... didn't know what to do ... " she began, but Traci angrily wadded her plastic-foam coffee cup and threw it toward the wastebasket.

"Fine. You explained. Now leave."

Ann turned, burning all over with humiliation, and walked out the door.

■

The next afternoon, Janene came by Ann's house.

"Ann, I've been at the hospital. Traci's dad has taken a turn for the worse. He may not pull through. Traci told me you and she had a fight, but I think she needs you. You're her best friend."

"Was," Ann corrected, her throat throbbing. "Janene, I've been thinking really hard. I like all of you so much, but you know as well as I do that we've been doing some stuff lately that could get any or all of us in trouble. Like stealing your father's car that night. What if we'd wrecked it?"

"We didn't steal it," Janene said quickly. "We just borrowed it for a while."

"Janene, if we'd asked permission to take it, he wouldn't have given it in a million years. Come on, this is the time for brutal honesty. We stole it. And we were just lucky we didn't get in trouble."

Janene sighed. "Okay, but what's that got to do with Traci?"

"My promise to lie for Trace was like the promises we've all seven made all along not to tell on each other. But this time, things got out of control. I feel guilty, but not for telling. I feel guilty for not being a good enough friend not to lie in the first place."

"Okay, I get your point. But what about Traci? She's too hurt and mixed up right now to think straight, but I know she needs to have you there with her."

"Then I'll go," Ann said softly. "But when this is over, no more lies. I won't do that anymore. Are you with me?"

Janene took a deep breath and headed for the door.

"Count on it," she said as they hurried out together.

The End

Ann's heart pounded so hard it hurt. Tara had made a real mistake. Of all the two-hundred-some juniors at Crestview High, she'd managed to pick someone that would just freeze up around her and would have no idea what to say or do.

"Sorry, but I've got to stay home today," Ann heard herself mumble. Boy, did that sound dumb.

"Oh, okay. Well, thanks anyway." Tara sounded truly disappointed. "Maybe another time."

Ann felt awful as she hung up the phone.

"But you just can't face going over there!" Ann scolded the blonde-haired girl that stood looking teary-eyed and helpless in her vanity mirror.

Well if you're never going to take chances then don't keep whining that you don't have any friends! responded a voice deep inside her.

She flopped back down on her bed and pulled her pillow tightly over her ears, but still the voice wouldn't shut up.

Take a chance! Call Tara back.

---

## What would you do?

*If Ann calls Tara, turn to page 10.*
*If she can't get up the nerve, turn to page 40.*

"I can't figure out what happened," Cora said, as the planners sat glumly after the so-called party was over. "I know everybody at school knew about this. Why did only four people show up?"

"Oh, everybody knew, all right." Randy shredded a plastic-foam cup in exasperation. "That was probably the whole trouble. They knew this was a church party, as opposed to the kegger going on over at Jack Fieldman's house tonight."

"Of course, we knew that kegger was going to be tonight, and we purposely scheduled this against it," Rachelle said thoughtfully. "Maybe next time, we should avoid doing that."

"Next time?" Keri Jones groaned.

"Well, if we do try this again ... and I said if ... I agree with what Rachelle's getting at," Cora said. "Let's put it on a night with nothing else going on. Even if they only come because we're the only party in town. Once everybody gets a taste of how much fun partying straight can be, they'll be lined up at the door for our third one."

"Third one?" Keri groaned again.

That cracked everybody up, and when the laughter died they were all feeling a little better.

"Try, try again," Jason Kyle murmured. "Who said that?"

"Porky Pig?" Randy guessed.

"Ben Franklin," Rachelle said firmly. "Or was it George Washington?"

"Who knows? The point is, whoever said it was right," Ann said softly. "We know how to do this now, so let's try it on another night. Besides, I ... well, I wouldn't say this was a total loss. I mean, I had a lot of fun planning it and putting it together with you guys."

"I'll drink to that," Jason said, raising a Coke.

"Who said 'I'll drink to that'?" asked Rachelle. "Moby Dick?"

"You're impossible. Just impossible," Ann giggled, then stood to help Randy dismantle the sound equipment 'til another time.

The End

As soon as Ann got home that evening, before she could lose her nerve, she called Tara and asked if she could stop by for a minute. Tara said yes, and when the two girls were settled in the den, Ann cleared her throat and dove in.

"Uh, Tara? I'm sorry I froze up on you when you started ... started to tell me about Jillian. You and she must have been really close, and I'd like to hear about her."

That opened the floodgates, and the quick stopover Ann had planned grew to two hours as Tara opened up about her life before her sister's death. And about her problems adjusting since then.

Over the next weeks, Ann listened many more times as Tara reminisced, sometimes with tears and sometimes with laughter.

"You've helped me so much, Ann," Tara told her one bright May day. "More than the counselor I had right after Jillian's death. Sometimes I wonder—why do you bother with me? I must be boring, with all my, well, problems and things."

"You're not boring!" Ann said quickly, with a laugh. "I like you Tara. And besides, it's like we learned in youth group. We're all supposed to help each other, like Jesus helped those around him while he was on Earth."

Tara nodded thoughtfully, and Ann had a sudden exciting idea.

"Tara, why don't you come with me to church and youth group? I bet you'd like it, and the kids would really love you!"

---

## Blind choice:
*Without looking ahead, turn to page 77 or page 87 to continue the story.*

"But heaven isn't only on Earth," Ann interjected, startled by her own boldness. "The Bible teaches that it's where believers can expect to spend eternity, after death."

Although Ann thought she'd just been stating the obvious, a deep silence followed, broken by a few snickers.

"Really, Ann," Desiree drawled, one side of her mouth drawn into a ridiculing smile. "This group is for creative minds, not for people bound to lazy, old-fashioned ways of thinking. The Bible is only one of many books of history and philosophy, no more and no less."

"The Hindu Upanashads contain some ideas for living that are much more relevant, in my opinion," said a boy across the circle.

"And the ancient oriental writings of Lao-tzu teach a more gentle, serene lifestyle," said another. "After all, the Bible and Christianity precipitated the Crusades, and the witch trials of the 16th century—two of the bloodiest events in history."

Ann wondered if anyone there had really read the Bible and studied the powerful, life-affirming message of Jesus. And how could they say Christianity had caused those events, when obviously they had gone so counter to Jesus' message of love?

She felt embarrassed and confused. A part of her just wanted to run from there, but a part of her said to relax. What was the big deal? Words couldn't hurt her—no matter how strange they were—so why didn't she just sit back and play along?

The air was thick with sweet-smelling smoke now, and Ann began to feel lightheaded. Leave or relax—she had to do one or the other fast.

## What would you do?

*If Ann leaves the meeting, turn to page 112.*
*If she settles back and relaxes, turn to page 81.*

"Tara, you can't do that!" Ann whispered urgently, running up and grabbing Tara's elbow.

"Do what?" Tara jerked her arm away. "Hey, back off, Ann. Get a grip."

"Put the necklaces back, please!"

"Listen!" Tara grabbed the front of Ann's jacket and bent to hiss angrily in her face. "Will you shut up and cool it before you get us both in trouble? I took one for you too, in case you didn't notice. So quit being such a baby."

"Put them back, Tara." Ann's heart was slamming, but she planted her feet and stood her ground.

"Just bug off," Tara spat out. "I can't believe I actually thought you and I could be friends."

Tara strode, fuming, from the store and quickly disappeared into the crowd. Ann didn't try to follow. But a few seconds later, when her brain thawed a little, she realized she was stranded four miles from home with no transportation. Mom was at work and couldn't pick her up. She didn't have money for a taxi.

What could she do?

"Ann? Hey, girl, what's wrong?"

Rachelle Washington, one of the kids in youth group, happened to be passing the store where Ann stood fighting back tears. Ann explained her situation, and Rachelle immediately offered her a ride home.

"This is really nice of you," Ann said, when they were settled in Rachelle's blue Tempo.

"Don't mention it." Rachelle waved a hand nonchalantly in the air. "I was going out to your neighborhood anyway when I finished shopping. There's a party I'm invited to a few blocks from your house—at Jamie White's."

She looked toward Ann.

"Hey, I've got an idea. Why don't you come with me? I mean, if you don't like the party, it's close enough for you to walk home. What do you say?"

"Oh, I don't think they'd want me," Ann said, her self-consciousness automatically kicking in.

"Listen, girl," Rachelle said, pushing her dark hair back behind her ears. "Don't worry about that. Everyone will like you just fine. Let's just go to the party and have fun, okay?"

Ann smiled and nodded. "Okay, sounds like fun."

■

It was dark in Jamie's house—all the curtains were pulled, and there was lots of smoke. You could tell in a flash there were no adults anywhere around—too many couples openly necking for that. One corner displayed a big cooler full of beer, and another provided the backdrop for a huge stereo system that throbbed out walls of sound.

Ann, who'd worried driving over that she wouldn't know what to say to the kids in Rachelle's crowd, realized that was one worry she could cross off her list. It was far too loud in here for anything resembling conversation.

James Harper came over, put his arm around Rachelle's shoulders and led her away. She looked back at Ann and shot her a "sorry but I'll see you later" smile. A few seconds later, Peter Thompson came up and leaned against the part of the wall where Ann was trying miserably to dissolve into the woodwork. He bent close to her, winked and held up his beer.

"Want one?" he mouthed.

## What would you do?

*If Ann decides to make an escape, turn to page 112.*
*If she accepts the beer and stays awhile, turn to page 53.*

"Thanks for inviting me, Tara, but I was going to invite you to spend the weekend with me. That way you could meet my mom, and we could see a movie or something Saturday. And Sunday you could come to Sunday school and go to youth group with me again."

Tara wrinkled her nose. "No offense, Ann, but you take all this church stuff way too seriously. I mean, church is okay when there's nothing else going on. I guess it's better than being totally bored. But this weekend, I really want to go to the lake. Maybe you can come with me some other time."

With a nonchalant wave, she left the car.

Ann felt let down. They'd had so much fun at the pizza party, and she'd really let herself hope that Tara would be a good friend. But suddenly, she didn't know how to relate to her at all.

Her confusion over Tara's attitude bothered her over the next few days—a lot. So much that during Sunday school, she decided to share her feelings.

"Have you ever had a friend who didn't believe like you believe?" she asked while everyone was chatting before beginning the lesson. "I mean, have you had a close friend who, well, put down your beliefs? Like they thought church was pretty unimportant? Kind of a waste of time?"

Everybody turned toward her, interested. Rachelle Washington frowned and scratched her ear.

"I dated a guy once who said he was an atheist," she murmured. "He just said that to get attention, I think. Still, it was hard listening to him talk that way. I didn't date him for long. He made me nervous."

"Yeah," Randy agreed. "It makes you feel uneasy, being around non-Christians who think it's cool to knock your faith. It's like people see you with them, and your own witness suffers."

"But on the other hand, how can you witness to non-Christians if you avoid them?" Jason asked softly, his gray eyes meeting Ann's. "If you only have Christian friends, you never have a chance to witness your faith in Christ."

"I guess you've got to figure out if the relationships are making them stronger or you weaker," Janene Grant added. "If your witness can bring them strength, then great. But if they're pulling you down and into weird stuff, forget it."

Ann thought about the times she'd been with Tara. She

thought of the invitation to the youth group Tara had enthusiastically accepted, then the embarrassing entrance she'd made and
what had happened afterward. On the other hand, Tara was
friendly and open, and had gone out of her way to invite Ann's
friendship.

Ann wondered—taken altogether—what did these things
mean? Was her relationship with Tara starting out to be healthy or
unhealthy?

## What would you do?

*If Ann decides the relationship is healthy, turn to page 52.*
*If she decides it's unhealthy, turn to page 93.*

Ann decided her new friends would help her through all this. Though they'd talked on a pretty flip, superficial level, Ann felt they'd surely get serious and support her if she needed it.

They were around their table in the cafeteria, when Ann, her heart beating fast, grabbed an empty moment to tell the others about her father's death.

"Wow, that's really a bummer, Ann," Heather Randolph said, dipping a fry in ketchup and drawing a smiley face on her tray with it. "I mean, you must be kind of like, sad, right?"

"Yeah, that's tough," Hillary added. "I felt awful when my grandmother died. She didn't leave me anything!"

The others spurted laughter at that.

"Oh, geeze, Hill—not even a piggy bank?" Jennifer Stewart drawled sarcastically. Hillary made a sarcastic face in return.

"Think of it, Ann," Tara said. "Maybe your dad had a will or something, and maybe you were in it. I mean, right, it's sad. But try to look at the bright side is all I'm saying. I mean, you don't want to walk around being all gloomy, do you?"

"No, sure. Thanks." Ann started collecting her things. "Will you guys excuse me? I've got to run into the science room and check on my experiment."

In the restroom, Ann locked herself into a stall and leaned against the door, crying silently. She'd never stopped to think that she might need friends she could really depend on someday. She'd fooled herself into thinking the popular girls were friends, when actually not one of them could think of anyone else or anything else but her own personal status in the school hierarchy. Ann had never felt so miserably alone.

"Ann?" There was a soft knock on the stall door. "Ann, it's Rachelle. Are you okay? I saw you run out of the cafeteria, and I was worried."

"Go away," Ann whispered.

Rachelle's voice was bringing back memories of how she'd felt with the youth group kids. Feelings of really belonging and being respected for who she was. Feelings of being a person, not a robot who had to perform all the time no matter how she felt.

"Ann, can't you talk about it?"

Shame and misery swirled inside Ann. "I ... I've been a real jerk to you, Rachelle. I don't ... don't deserve for you to worry about me."

"But I do," Rachelle said simply.

Ann dried her eyes on a piece of toilet paper and slowly opened the door.

Rachelle reached out and hugged Ann for a long time. Ann just clung to her, crying. After several minutes, Ann got up the courage to pull away from Rachelle and look at her. She wanted to explain what had happened and apologize for shunning the kids at church. But when she looked at Rachelle, all her fears drained right out of her, along with her words.

Rachelle reached down and took the piece of toilet paper Ann was holding, smiled, then wiped the tears from her own eyes. Ann couldn't believe it. Rachelle had been crying too—for Ann.

But somehow, Ann thought, Rachelle's tears were just as much from joy as from compassion.

The End

"It was okay," Ann answered, not meeting Mom's eyes. "By the way, before I forget, we're going again next weekend."

She'd purposely phrased that as a statement instead of a question. After all, she felt years older than she had before this weekend, so why should Mom be able to boss her around?

The next Saturday, when Tara honked outside, Ann ran to meet her without looking back to catch Mom's disapproving gaze.

"Hop in! We have one more stop before we go," Tara giggled. "We have to get the surprise I told you about."

Minutes later Tara stopped at an unfamiliar house and Roger and Tim came bounding into the car—with their bags.

"Surprise!" yelled Tara, grinning.

The four of them were soon on their way out of town, the radio blaring and the trunk full of beer and suntan oil.

■

Late that afternoon, the foursome took the boat across to The Cove, a club at the lake's edge.

"Won't they card us?" Ann asked worriedly.

"Nah." Tara threw a T-shirt over her bikini. "My parents are members here, and they don't card members' kids."

They entered the dark building without being stopped, and soon Tara and Roger were swaying on the dance floor to the slow, seductive music. Tim pulled Ann out of the booth they'd shared and onto the dance floor. He pulled her close to him too.

After half an hour, Tara laughingly pried Ann loose and drug her into the restroom for a conference.

"This is going so great!" she sighed, studying herself in the mirror and wiping off a smudge of mascara. "My folks and their friends are dancing in town and won't be back 'til way into the morning, so we'll have the house to ourselves!" She winked in the mirror at Ann. "Roger and I have dibs on the master bedroom."

Ann was stunned. Despite the bags they toted, Ann had hoped the boys would go home tonight. But she was stranded too far from home to do much about it. And Tim *was* cute.

## What would you do?

*If Ann goes along with Tara's plan for the night, turn to page 44.*
*If she tries to change Tara's mind instead, turn to page 58.*

All the next week, Ann tried to get up her nerve, but the most she could manage was a friendly smile when she saw Tara at school. She just couldn't bring herself to dial the phone to invite Tara over.

The week after that, the problem had grown a little dimmer in her mind, and by the end of a month, she'd decided Tara must've linked up with other people by now. Probably she'd found someone who could comfort her and help her get past her grief for Jillian. Someone more suitable, stronger than Ann. Better at it.

School let out for summer break, and Ann got a job helping coach the children's tennis program. That kept her so busy she didn't think of Tara at all. Then one hot July night, riffling through the Crestview Herald News for the crossword puzzle, Ann saw Tara's obituary. The black letters swam before her eyes, and her ears rang.

Drowned. Family pool. Drowned.

A haze settled over Ann and grew thicker in the following days. Around town, people were calling Tara's awful death a suicide. A vision of Tara by the pool, a wine cooler in her hand, seared like acid into Ann's frozen brain, and she kept hearing Tara's voice that morning at her house—"... sometimes I just want to end things ... end things ..."

Ann avoided the question as long as she could, but finally, after many sleepless nights, she had to ask herself—was Tara's death suicide? And could she have helped before it was too late?

## What would you do?

*If Ann blames herself for Tara's suicide, turn to page 36.*
*If she decides she couldn't have helped Tara anyway, turn to page 55.*

"Uh, I don't, uh, think I can, Tara," Ann stammered. "Thanks for inviting me, though."

She felt miserably embarrassed at not giving an excuse, but she couldn't think of one on the spur of the moment like this.

And something else happened that drove any germ of an idea for an excuse far from her brain. At first she thought her eyes were playing tricks on her. But no—there hadn't been a mistake. The display case that had held five necklaces now held three.

Tara had just nonchalantly pocketed two of the gold chains she'd been fingering for the last few minutes.

"Okay," Tara said with a bored yawn. "Suit yourself, Ann."

She began walking coolly from the store, while Ann stared at Tara's back, frozen in shock.

Tara had just shoplifted two necklaces! Somebody had to stop her, and the only "somebody" around was Ann! But how could she get up enough nerve to do that?

## What would you do?

*If Ann confronts Tara about the theft, turn to page 120.*
*If she stays quiet, turn to page 130.*

She wanted to run up and confront Tara, to tell her to put the chains back, but she couldn't find the courage. So she just followed her from the store, feeling numb with mortification.

"Not so fast, girls." A security guard just outside the shop stepped forward to block their path. "We have everything on video. You two will have to come to the office with me."

■

The hour waiting in the mall manager's office for Mom to come from work to pick her up was the worst hour of Ann's life. The lecture from two police officers called by the security guard was humiliating enough, but she dreaded even more the look of disappointment and shock she knew would be on her mother's face.

Tara's father arrived first and took her away after rudely telling the policemen they should be out arresting *real* criminals.

Mom, on the other hand, arrived looking confused and worried, and apologized to the officers for the trouble they'd taken.

In the car, Mom was straightforward.

"All right, Annie. Tell me what happened. Exactly."

Through tears of shame, Ann told her, omitting nothing, not even the way she'd tried too hard to impress Tara.

"Annie, you just have to learn to stand up for yourself and not be so easily led. Your lack of self-confidence is always going to make you easy prey to everybody's bad ideas."

"I know," Ann whispered.

■

By Monday morning, Ann had more or less put the awful episode behind her. But when she walked into the school, it didn't take her long to find out that the newest hot scuttlebutt going around was about her. It seemed Tara was telling everybody who'd listen that it was **Ann** who'd stolen the necklaces and gotten them arrested at the mall.

Ann felt sick and wondered how to respond.

## What would you do?

*If Ann reacts with anger, turn to page 68.*
*If Ann decides to just ignore this, turn to page 88.*

"Well, their place is beautiful," Ann began, flopping down on the couch and kicking off her tennis shoes. "And they've got a great boat. I was going to ski some, but ... well, you know. We did other things."

"Oh. Like?"

Ann took a deep breath. "Roger and Tim, two guys from school, came by."

Mom's eyebrows shot up.

"And, well, you might as well know. There was a little drinking. The adults were doing it, so the boys and Tara had a few beers too. I didn't, of course."

"Annie," Mom sounded stern. "I wouldn't have given you permission to go if I'd known boys would be there. And drinking? I don't like this a bit. Not one bit."

"But it was so fun, and I know better than to do anything stupid and get in trouble," Ann automatically protested, jiggling one foot nervously.

"Honey, sometimes you really can't control situations. Sometimes you just have to use your head and avoid them in the first place. Now Tara seems to be one of those people who's used to always getting her own way, and friends like that can be hard to stand up to."

"So you're saying I can't go to the lake house again?" Ann mumbled.

"Before I answer, you answer a question. Can you tell me, honestly, that you and Tara will be there alone without the boys or the beer, and that you'll be able to say no to any silly and dangerous idea she comes up with?"

Ann licked her lips, but the words wouldn't come out.

"Okay, Mom, you're right," she finally said. "I won't go to the lake. But I still want to try to be friends with Tara."

Mom nodded, looking relieved, and reached over to pat her leg. "Just remember who you are, and that your values are more important than anyone else's scatterbrained plans."

■

When Ann said she couldn't go to the lake the next week, Tara invited Hillary Stanton, the leader of the popular group at school instead. After that, Tara began running around with Hillary's gang. She was still friendly to Ann in the halls at school, though, and to Ann's surprise, one day Hillary herself came up and invited her to a party at her house.

"It's Sunday night," Hillary told her. "Hope you can come. Tara said she'd pick you up."

Ann was taken by surprise. Surely everybody dreamed of being included by the popular crowd. But lately, Ann had been getting close to a few of the kids in youth group, and she really hated to miss Sunday night. This particular Sunday night, in fact, she was even in charge of part of the program.

## What would you do?

*If she goes to Hillary's party, turn to page 63.*
*If she decides to pass, turn to page 72.*